Sphere Of Untrodden Learning

OrangeBooks Publication

1st Floor, Rajhans Arcade, Mall Road, Kohka, Bhilai, Chhattisgarh 490020

Website: **www.orangebooks.in**

First Edition, 2025

ISBN: 978-93-7426-110-1

Price: Rs. 350.00

Printed in India

SPHERE OF UNTRODDEN LEARNING

DISCOVER THE GLOW WITHIN

Orange Books Publication
www.orangebooks.in

Preface

In a world that moves faster each day, where noise often drowns out clarity and expectations overshadow self-worth, we find ourselves asking a simple question: "*What truly matters?*"

This book is my humble attempt to answer that for anyone who has ever paused in the middle of their busy life and wondered if there's something more. Through years of reflection, observation, and personal practice, I came to realise that the journey inward is just as important as the journey forward.

Within these pages, you'll find thoughts and reflections on calmness, self-awareness, purpose, and the small yet powerful habits that help shape a meaningful life. You'll discover the concept of "Atoms", fundamental elements like Health, Knowledge, and Calmness that, when aligned, create a unique inner glow, visible to the world.

This book is to explore a question that has quietly echoed through many hearts, asking Is there something more to life than just motion and achievement?

It's written for anyone who has ever stopped, even for a fleeting moment, in the middle of their busy days and felt a gentle nudge from within with an inner whisper asking, *"Is this all there is?"*

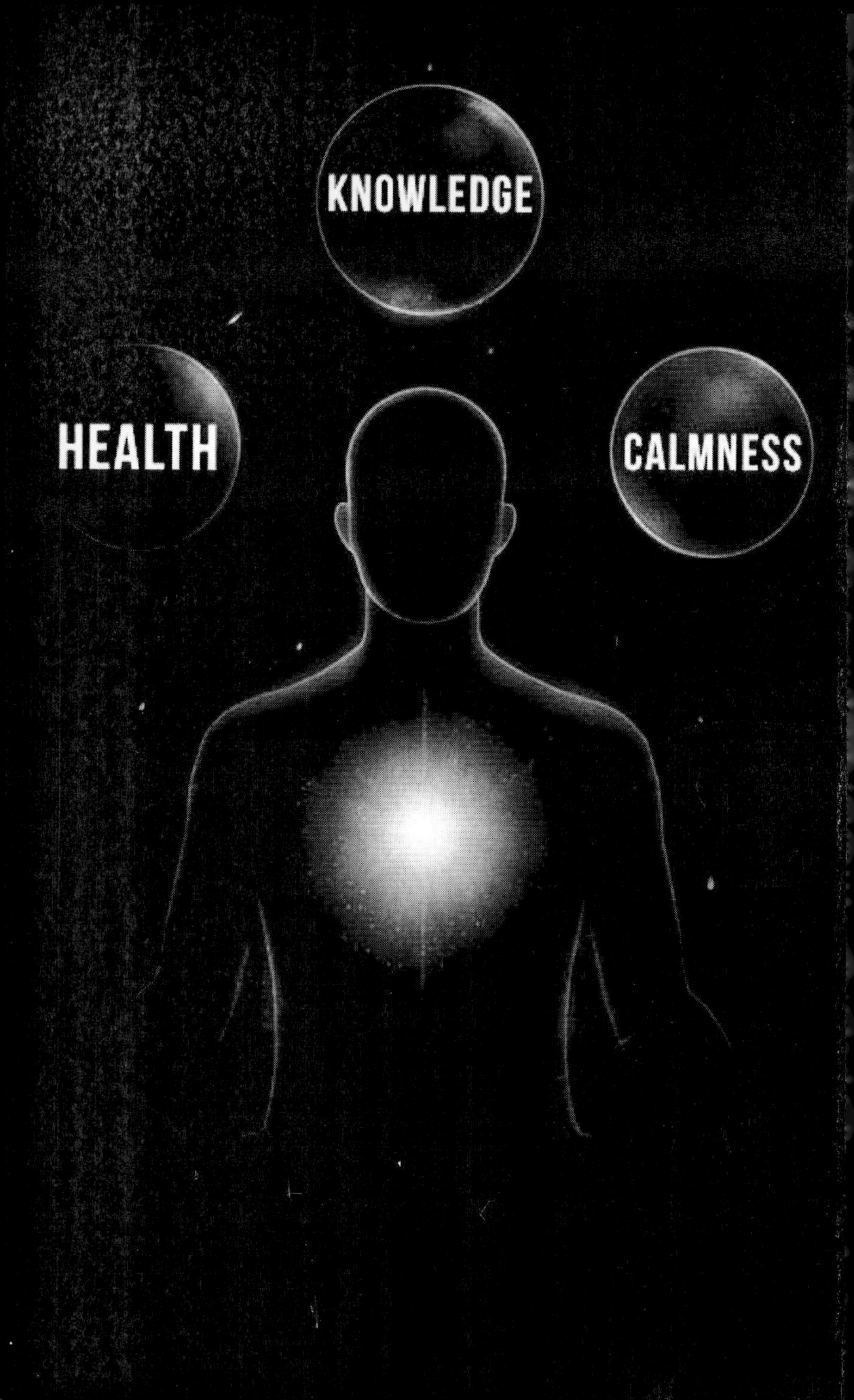
KNOWLEDGE
HEALTH
CALMNESS

Over the years, through moments of silence, countless observations, and deliberate personal practices, I have come to realise something profound that the journey inward is not separate from the journey forward. It is the compass that gives it direction.

This book doesn't promise all the answers. Instead, it invites you to slow down and reflect, to question and to listen.

Within these pages, you'll find a blend of reflections and gentle guidance on the nature of calmness, the power of self-awareness, the pursuit of purpose, and the quiet strength of everyday habits that can lead to a truly meaningful life.

At the heart of it lies the core idea of **"Atoms"**, invisible forces like **Health, Knowledge, and Calmness**. These are not merely ideas or practices; instead, they are energetic building blocks. When nurtured and brought into harmony, they begin to collide and fuse, creating a luminous inner glow, a presence, a radiance that doesn't need to be spoken to be felt.

This glow, I believe, is already within you. This book is simply a mirror to help you see it more clearly.

This book is not a rulebook. It is a companion. A guide. A mirror. It invites you to explore your own beliefs, your daily choices, your moments of doubt, and your hidden strength. I've used stories, affirmations, and real-life insights to connect ideas with action, so this isn't just something you read, but something you live.

I would take a moment to express my deepest gratitude to my family. Your love, patience, and constant encouragement have been my foundation. You gave me the space to think, the strength to write, and the belief that my words matter. Every chapter is touched by your presence, every page shaped by your support. I am also deeply grateful to Haritosh Srivastav, as it was during one of his powerful challenge sessions that I discovered the spark and inspiration to begin writing my book. His guidance and thought-provoking approach opened a new perspective for me, and that moment became the turning point where the idea of putting my thoughts into a book truly took shape.

My only hope is that while going through these pages, you rediscover your own story and begin telling it with greater honesty, confidence, and joy.

Welcome to your journey back to yourself.

Index

Part - 3

Living Radiantly And Sharing The Light

PART - 1

UNDERSTANDING YOUR INNER GLOW

Chapter 1

The Pulse Beneath All Things

At some point in life, most people stop and ask themselves some very big questions:

- Why am I here?
- What is the purpose of my life?
- What should I be doing?
- Why do I feel like something is missing?
- Where can I truly make a difference?

These questions don't always come loudly. Sometimes, they quietly echo in the back of our minds, especially when we are alone or going through a hard time. We hope that maybe one day, someone will help us find the answers—perhaps a teacher, a friend, a wise person, or even a book like this one.

But the truth is that only you can find your own answers. Other people can guide you, inspire you, or walk with you on the journey, but they cannot look inside your heart. They don't know your dreams, your struggles, your emotions, or your life story the way you do.

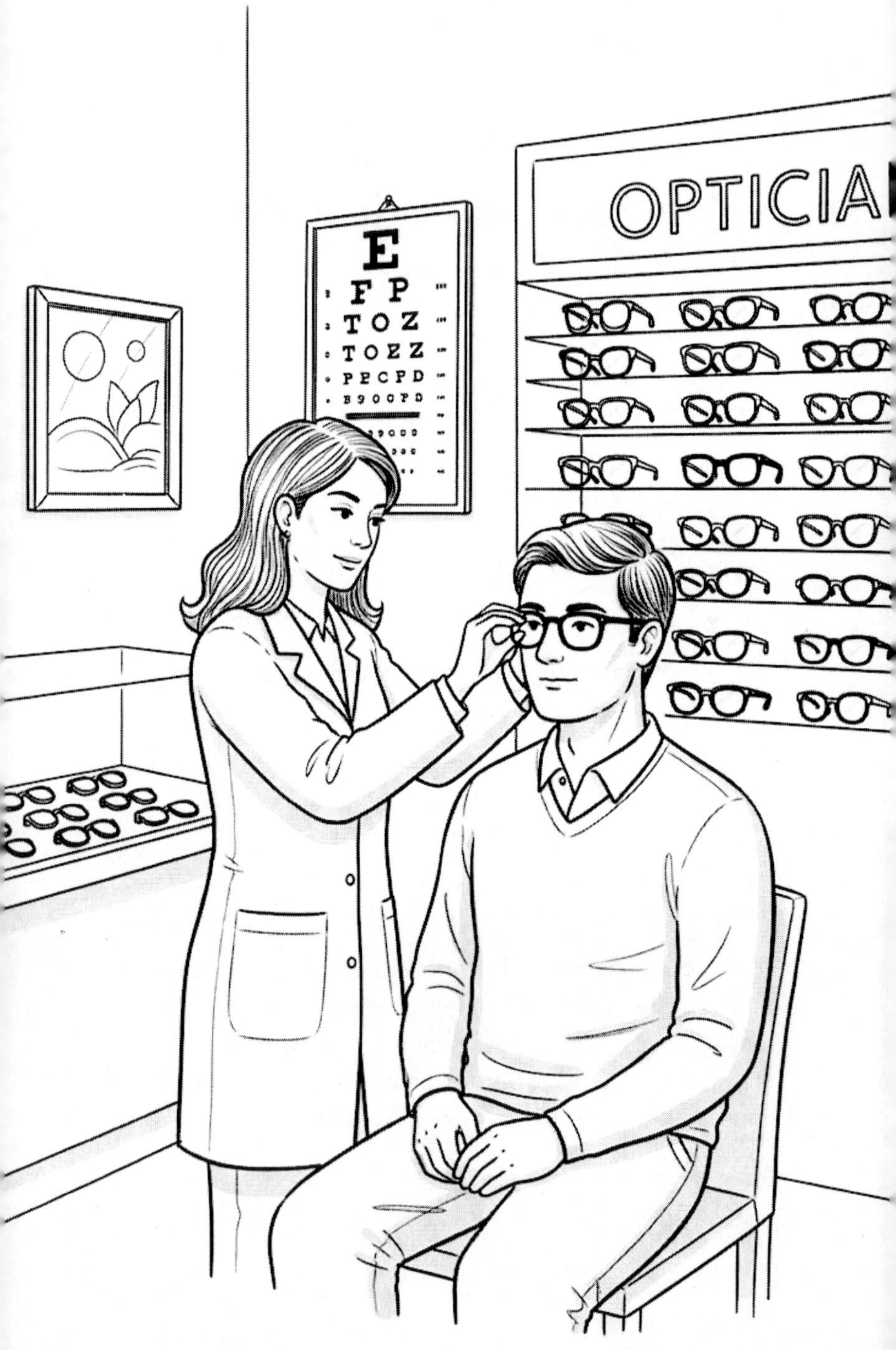
OPTICIA
E
F P
T O Z

Me Visiting Ophthalmologist

Recently, I visited an ophthalmologist for a new pair of glasses. The doctor shone a light into my eyes, asked me to read letters from a chart, and then placed different lenses in front of me.

"Is this clearer? Or this one?" the doctor asked as the lenses shifted.

At first, both options looked similar. Sometimes the difference was obvious, and other times I had to pause and really notice what felt right. The ophthalmologist guided me, but ultimately, the decision rested with me. The doctor could not look through my eyes. Only I could determine which lens brought the world into sharper focus.

Life's purpose works in much the same way.

Many people, like family, friends, teachers, and mentors will suggest what they think is best for you. They may offer advice with love, wisdom, and even good experience behind it. But no matter how well - meaning they are, they cannot live inside your skin. They cannot see the world through your eyes or feel it through your heart. Only you can decide which "lens" makes your life meaningful, and which path brings your vision into focus.

Your life's purpose is not a formula someone else can hand over to you. It isn't something you can borrow, copy, or download like an app. It is deeply personal, which is shaped by your experiences, your struggles, your values, and your dreams. Just as no two fingerprints are alike, no two life purposes are identical.

Uncovering this purpose is not a one-time event. It's more like polishing a mirror or adjusting those lenses at the eye clinic gradually, little by little, the picture becomes clearer. Sometimes clarity comes after years of confusion. Other times, it emerges in sudden flashes of insight when you least expect it.

Finding your purpose is rarely easy. In fact, many people spend a long time searching. You might not know where to begin. You might feel lost, overwhelmed, or even doubtful that a purpose exists for you at all. That's perfectly normal.

The truth is, the starting point is always right where you are. Whether you're in a season of uncertainty, burnout, curiosity, or quiet longing, that very state is not the end; instead it's the beginning. Your feelings of confusion are simply signals that you are ready to explore, to look inward, and to listen more closely.

Your mission is yours alone. It doesn't have to look like anyone else's. It doesn't have to impress or prove anything to the world. It simply has to feel true to you.

And when you begin to live aligned with that inner clarity, life itself starts to feel sharper, richer, and more meaningful, just as the world looks brighter and more defined when you finally put on the right pair of glasses.

Your life's purpose is not given to you; it is discovered by you. Others can guide, but only you can choose the lens through which your life becomes clear.

So how do you begin to uncover your purpose? One way is to notice the small but powerful clues that life keeps offering you.

- **What brings you joy?** Those moments when you lose track of time because you are so absorbed in what you're doing.
- **What makes you feel alive?** The activities or conversations that leave you energised rather than drained.
- **What stirs your compassion?** The issues, causes, or problems in the world that tug at your heart.
- **What occupies your thoughts?** The ideas or dreams you return to, again and again, even when you're busy with something else.

These are not random; instead, they are guideposts pointing you toward what matters most.

Your mission is yours alone. It doesn't have to look like anyone else's. It doesn't have to impress or prove anything to the world. It simply has to feel true to you.

And when you begin to live aligned with that inner clarity, life itself starts to feel sharper, richer, and more meaningful, just as the world looks brighter and more defined when you finally put on the right pair of glasses.

Your life's purpose is not given to you; it is discovered by you. Others can guide, but only you can choose the lens through which your life becomes clear.

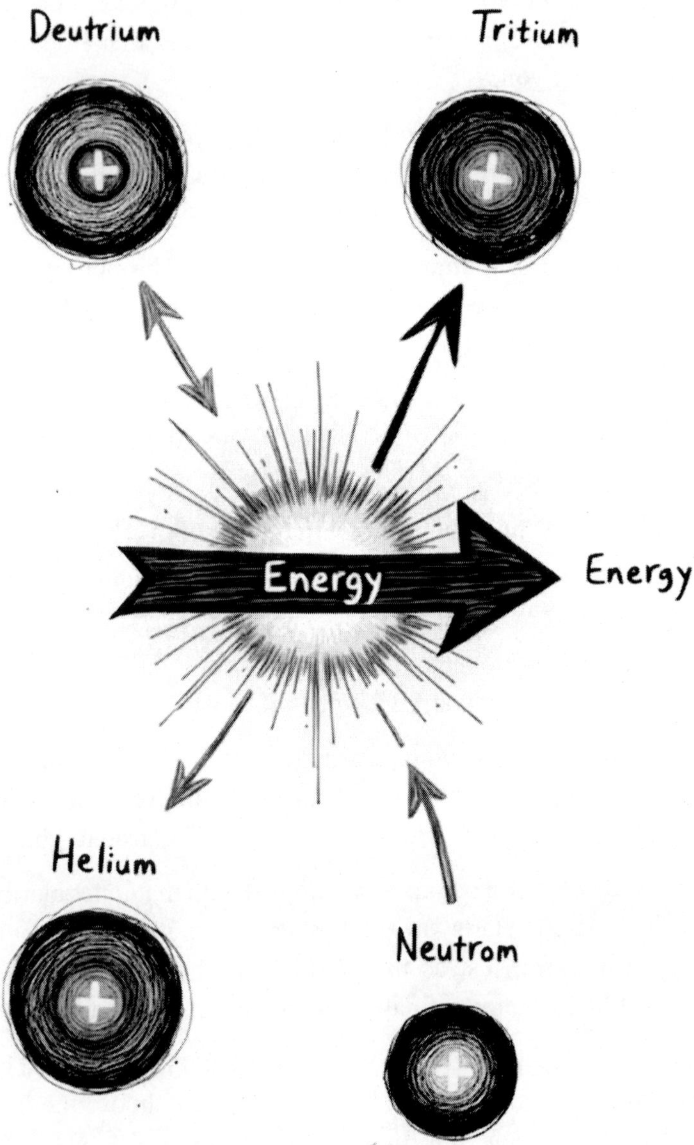

Deutrium
Tritium
Energy
Energy
Helium
Neutrom

Fusion Reaction – Igniting Your Inner Sun

Let's go back to school science for a moment. Do you recall a fascinating concept called **nuclear fusion**?

Fusion is a process where two small atoms, like hydrogen, come close together and join to form a bigger atom, like helium. When they combine, they create a huge amount of energy. This is the reaction that powers the Sun. Yes, the Sun, the big ball of fire that lights up the sky and gives us warmth and life.

Now, why are we talking about the Sun and atoms in a book about life and happiness?

Because this powerful fusion can happen inside you, too.

Think about it. Each of us has many fragmented parts, like our memories, beliefs, emotions, experiences, struggles, successes, fears, dreams, values, and even our failures. Often, these pieces feel scattered, disconnected, or even in conflict. But when you begin to bring these parts together and when your thoughts align with your values, your dreams embrace your scars, and your wisdom learns from your pain, something profound begins to happen.

That's your inner fusion, a power coming together of your authentic self.

And just like nuclear fusion creates light and energy in the Sun, this internal fusion creates clarity, confidence, strength, and deep joy within you. It becomes your own personal Sun radiating from within, guiding your path, and warming your life even on the darkest days.

Let's pause here and look at a few concepts we often take for granted. Almost everyone aspires to live a good life, one that is healthy, wealthy, and wise. But let's take a closer look at what those words often mean in our current world:

- **Health** often just means "not being sick."
- **Wealth** is usually measured by how much money or how many things we have.
- **Wisdom** is seen as having information or being clever.

Even if you possess all three, i.e. health, wealth, and wisdom, there is still no guarantee you will be happy. You might have a strong body, a comfortable lifestyle, and a sharp mind, yet still feel an unexplainable emptiness inside. That's because true happiness is something much deeper.

It isn't just about having a reason to laugh at parties or showing off cheerful snapshots on social media. Those moments may look bright on the outside, but they are often temporary, like fireworks that dazzle for a second and fade into the dark sky. Real happiness is more like a steady flame which is quiet, glowing, and deeply rooted. It's a sense of inner peace and fulfilment that stays with you no matter what happens around you.

Here's the most beautiful truth that happiness multiplies when it is shared. Unlike material possessions, which shrink when divided, happiness expands. When you smile at your family, comfort a friend, help a neighbour, or show kindness to a stranger, you don't lose anything; in fact, you gain more.

Think about a candle. If one candle lights another, the first candle doesn't burn out; instead, the room becomes brighter. The same happens with happiness. Every time you share a piece of it, it grows stronger within you, creating a ripple effect that touches lives beyond your imagination.

But if happiness is such a natural gift, why do so many people struggle to find it? One reason is the pace of today's world. Life moves at lightning speed. Work deadlines pile up, family responsibilities stretch us thin, digital distractions flood our attention, and social expectations whisper that we must keep achieving, posting, and proving ourselves.

The result? Life feels loud, cluttered, and demanding. In all this noise, true happiness becomes harder to hear. We chase it, but it feels like a mirage.

When boredom, anxiety, or sadness strike, most of us instinctively reach for quick escapes. We stream endless shows, scroll through social media for hours, binge shop online, or drown ourselves in food, gossip, or entertainment.

These activities may give us a temporary high. They numb our worries for a while, but once the distraction fades, the same old emptiness returns. It's like drinking salt water when you're thirsty. It feels satisfying for a moment, but in the end, it leaves you even more dehydrated.

Why does this happen? Because lasting happiness doesn't live outside of us. It is not something to chase, purchase, or consume. External pleasures can support happiness, but they cannot create it.

Me Cooking

Let me explain with an example from cooking. If I want to make a tasty dish, I need the right ingredients. I also need to follow a good recipe. I can't just throw random things in a pot and expect it to taste good.

Life is the same. If you want a life full of happiness and peace, you need to understand the ingredients like kindness, clarity, gratitude, self-awareness and follow a process. You can't just rush through life and hope everything works out.

This book will show you that process. Think of it as your happiness recipe. Step by step, we will look at how to understand yourself better, build healthy habits, and bring together the powerful parts of your personality just like a fusion reaction.

Inside you is a light, like the Sun. Right now, it may be small or hidden. But it is there.

As we go through this book, we'll explore ideas and stories that act like the heat in a fusion reaction. They will warm up your thoughts and feelings, helping you find your purpose. We'll also look at the life-elements inside you, like your fears, dreams, talents, and values and show how, when they come together, they can create real energy and happiness.

When this fusion happens, you will not just shine for yourself but for everyone around you.

Begin by asking simple questions:

- What really matters to me?
- What makes me feel alive?
- What kind of person do I want to become?

Don't worry if the answers don't come right away. Keep asking. Keep listening. The answers are already inside you. You just need to slow down, pay attention, and trust the process.

So let me begin by wishing you this:

Let me end this chapter with a small wish for you.

May your inner light shine brightly. May your personal Sun never fade. And may this journey help you discover the beautiful, powerful fusion that lives inside you.

Let's begin. The journey to your own happiness starts now.

Key Takeaways

- Your life's purpose is as distinctive as your fingerprint. No one else can live it but you.
- True happiness goes beyond just being happy, healthy, or wise. It's a deeper alignment with your inner self.
- When your inner purpose and energy align, you don't just glow instead, you become a light for others.

Notes

Chapter 2

The Silent Strength Within

When we hear the word health, most of us instantly think of the basics, i.e. physical fitness, proper nutrition, and mental wellness. And yes, each of these pillars is incredibly important. They're the foundation of how we function, feel, and experience life.

But health is often something we take for granted until it's gone.

I often think back to my childhood. Like most kids, I had my share of illnesses, like high fevers that made my body ache, days spent in bed coughing and sneezing, and feeling weak and restless. Those moments felt endless. I would lie there, wondering when I would feel normal again. But then, as children do, I would recover quickly. A few days later, I would be running, laughing, and playing again, bursting with energy, as if the sickness had never happened. It's only in those small windows of illness that we truly understand how precious good health is.

Even something as routine as a cold can remind us how fragile and vital our well-being truly is. One moment, we are rushing through our daily tasks, and the next, a simple fever or sore throat can bring everything to a sudden halt.

It interrupts our plans, slows our pace, and demands that we step back from our usual rhythm. In those quiet, uncomfortable pauses, we are forced to rest, reflect, and reset. But not all illnesses are temporary.

Hospitals Full of Patients

In 2022, our lives changed forever. That was the year my uncle was diagnosed with Chronic Kidney Disease (CKD). What followed was a journey filled with uncertainty, fear, and relentless effort. I stood by his side through countless hospital visits, OPD consultations, room admissions, and long hours in intensive care units. Every day felt like a battle with medication, with decisions, and most of all, with time. Despite all our efforts and hopes, we lost him. It was heart breaking. The pain of losing a loved one is indescribable. But even amidst the grief, something else began to take root in my mind, a disturbing realisation.

During those hospital visits, I saw something I wasn't prepared for. I had always thought hospitals were filled mostly with elderly patients suffering from age-related illnesses. But what I saw shook me deeply. Children, school - going kids were lying in ICU beds, battling illnesses I had barely even heard of. Some were hooked up to dialysis machines. These were children who should have been playing in parks, going to school, laughing, and living a carefree life. Instead, they were fighting for survival.

That sight left a lasting scar on my heart. This made me realise that something fundamental is going wrong. Health issues that once seemed distant or age-related are now affecting the youngest among us. It's a wake-up call.

We need to reflect on our lifestyles, environment, and systems, and take action to correct what has gone wrong before it's too late.

If you ask me what's driving this silent health crisis, the first thing that comes to mind is the drastic shift in our food habits and lifestyle choices.

The rise of fast - food culture, the dominance of processed meals, and the explosive growth of food delivery apps have completely transformed the way we eat. It's convenient, fast, and, for many, almost addictive. These services fit perfectly into our busy, fast-paced lives where time feels scarce and instant gratification is rewarded. Well question is not to demonise outside food or claim that ordering out will instantly ruin your health. Life is all about balance and joy, too. The concern arises when these shortcuts become the norm instead of the exception.

When children can instantly recognise the logos of global fast-food chains yet struggle to name common vegetables, we have a problem. When a family dinner is more likely to involve scrolling through a delivery app than cooking together, something fundamental is being lost. Slowly, we replace not just the nutrition of home-cooked meals but also the habits, values, and traditions that come with them.

This cultural shift doesn't reveal its consequences overnight. It doesn't shout; it whispers. The late-night cravings, the skipped breakfasts, the endless cycle of takeout dinners all feel harmless in the moment. But over time, these small choices accumulate. The convenience we celebrate today may quietly transform into the very reason we face chronic health struggles tomorrow.

Many of these struggles are preventable if only we paused to reflect on what's really fuelling our bodies and our lives.

Chain Smoking

I have a friend who is a chain smoker. Once, he had to go for a full health check-up with his family. He was extremely worried. He thought that if there were any signs of infection, his family would find out about his smoking habit. But to his surprise, all his reports came back normal.

He told me that even though he smokes a lot, he also has certain healthy habits, especially in terms of his diet. He regularly eats certain foods that help support his overall health. This made me realise something important that it's not always one bad habit that causes health issues. It is the overall lifestyle that makes the difference.

So, here's the point. Eating fast food isn't automatically harmful if we ensure two things. First, that the quality of the food is good, and second, that we balance it out with nutritious food. We need to create a diet that satisfies our taste buds and supports our health. Striking this balance is the key.

These days, there's a lot of talk on social media about how packed and processed foods contain harmful chemicals and artificial colours. Honestly, I don't want to go too deep into that debate as I'm not in a position to prove whether those claims are entirely true or not.

My submission is that if we can make chips at home, why buy the packaged ones from the market? If we can prepare chutneys at home, why not make our own ketchup too, instead of using bottled versions? Stick to homemade, healthy, and nutritious food as much as possible. Choose outside or packaged food only when it's truly necessary.

Your Glow Comes From Within

You might be wondering how being nutritious can help you find your glow or energy. The truth is, building that inner glow is like following a recipe; it takes a process, and good health is the foundation.

If we're constantly dealing with poor physical health, how can we focus on discovering our passion or reaching our goals? Our energy is often drained not because we're doing too much, but because our bodies aren't getting what they need to stay strong.

Start by correcting your food habits. This is one of the biggest reasons your energy might feel low. Eat nutritious meals, drink enough water, and most importantly, eat and drink with ease without focusing somewhere else. That moment should be totally focused without any external distractions. Our body needs time to digest the food and liquids we consume. Give it that time, and you'll begin to feel the difference.

There was a time when we drank water straight from taps or wells, no filters, no purifiers. Then came the era of water filters, followed by RO (Reverse Osmosis) systems. Now, we're being told that RO systems remove not just impurities, but also essential minerals from the water. So what's the solution? A new system that adds minerals back into the water.

This makes me wonder where we are really heading? First, we take minerals out, then we create a new technology to put them back in. Is this truly necessary, or is it just another marketing strategy? Honestly, I don't know. But I do feel that in today's world, people often follow whatever they see in advertisements or on social media, assuming it must be right.

I'm not saying that everything we see online is false. Many innovations are genuinely helpful. But at the same time, we shouldn't forget the basics. We should stay rooted in common sense and not blindly follow trends. Yes, the world is changing fast, and we should move along with it, but let's not lose sight of what's essential and natural in the process.

Think of your health as the first spark in creating your own *personal fusion reaction*, your inner source of energy, strength, and passion. That's why it deserves the highest priority in your life.

You're likely in one of two situations. Either you're living with a permanent health condition like high blood pressure, or you're not facing any major health issues right now.

If you're fortunate enough to be free from chronic illness, that's amazing! Use this time wisely. Start adopting healthy habits now so your body builds strong immunity and stays protected in the future.

But even if you're dealing with a long-term condition, don't lose hope. Along with the medications your doctor has prescribed, begin making small, healthy changes to your daily routine. It may take time, but it's possible to regain control over your energy and well-being.

No matter where you stand today, improving your health is the first and most important step in unlocking your full potential.

During my childhood, the concept of regular health check-ups was almost non-existent. It was something we rarely thought about. Now, we're constantly reminded that if we don't opt for periodic health screenings, we risk missing something critical. Ironically, the focus seems less on proactively staying healthy and more on catching potential permanent illnesses early. It's as if we're being conditioned to look for sickness rather than cultivating long-term wellness. Strange, isn't it?

In today's world, schools must take up the responsibility of instilling healthy habits in children from an early age. One of the most impactful ways to do this is by incorporating lessons on the benefits of nutritious food into the curriculum. If these lessons are taught in a fun, interactive manner through stories, activities, or games and if children are shown real-world consequences of regularly consuming packaged and junk food, they are more likely to understand the importance of healthy eating. These early realisations can shape a lifetime of good habits, influencing not just individual lives but entire communities over time.

The Five Monkeys and the Banana

Once upon a time, a group of scientists placed five monkeys in an enclosed chamber. At the top of the chamber, they hung a bunch of bananas and placed a ladder underneath. Naturally, a monkey spotted the bananas and started climbing the ladder to grab them.

But as soon as he did, the scientists sprayed all the monkeys with cold water.

Shivering and startled, the monkeys quickly learned to associate the act of climbing the ladder with punishment. Over time, every time one of them tried to climb, the others would physically stop him to avoid the unpleasant spray.

Then the scientists began replacing the original monkeys one by one. Each new monkey, unaware of the cold water, would instinctively try to reach the bananas only to be beaten down by the others. Even monkeys who had never experienced the water themselves began enforcing the behaviour. Eventually, all the original monkeys were replaced, yet none of the current group dared to go for the bananas, even though they had no idea why. It had simply become the norm.

This story is a powerful metaphor. That's why it's crucial to educate children about healthy living, not just with instructions, but with understanding and context. It may take time, but slowly, this awareness will spread like waves through families and communities, creating a cultural shift toward health and wellness.

My Strong Grandmother

Let me share a deeply personal example. My grandmother is 95 years old. She has been living with chronic conditions like high blood pressure and diabetes for decades. Recently, she has been experiencing severe leg pain, so much so that even walking has become a challenge. And yet, despite all this, I have never seen her in a state of emotional or mental distress.

She remains spirited, cheerful, and ever-eager to share stories from her life. Though she lives far from me, she insists we talk daily. Whenever I ask about her health, she replies with a Sindhi proverb: "Jian halaye tiyan wah wah", which translates to, “Whatever condition God wishes me to live in, I happily accept.”

Her firm acceptance and positive spirit are nothing short of inspiring. This, I believe, is the state of mind we must all strive for, one where inner peace transcends physical ailments. When we reach this level of resilience and grace, we attain what I like to call a “Health Atom”, a core of well-being and acceptance. This inner strength is what fuels our personal nuclear reaction, the energy and positivity we radiate to the world around us.

Your energy starts from within. Take care of your body, and it will take care of everything else.

Key Takeaways

- You can fuel your body with nourishment. Let wholesome, nutritious food be your daily ritual.
- Advantage of being focused while you eat. Honour your body's rhythm.
- Miracle of cultivating a 'Health Atom'. A powerful nucleus of habits that radiate vitality and wellness.

Practice Exercise

🎯 Practice 1: Daily Body Check-In (5 Minutes)

Each morning or evening, take 5 minutes to sit quietly and ask yourself:

1. **How does my body feel right now?** (Tired, tense, light, heavy, calm, energetic…)
2. **What does my body need today?** (Rest, more water, gentle movement, better food, quiet time…)
3. **Am I listening to my body or ignoring it?**

📝 *Write your answers in a small notebook or chart below. Identify why you feel like that? What small steps do you take to improve health bit by bit? No hurry, Health first, start mentally and then physically.*

Date:

Question	Response
Body Check-In	
Body's daily needs	
Body Awareness Check	
My Next Action	

🎯 Practice 2: 5 Simple Health Habits

- Give yourself comfortable time when eating food. No work, no television. Only time with yourself and your loved ones.
- Create your schedule for eating food and follow it.
- Walk or stretch for 30–45 minutes daily.
- Follow a sleep schedule which keeps you active when you wake up. Keep on altering the schedule until you identify your comfortable schedule.
- Silence for 2 minutes whenever you feel stressed.

Circle or write down the habits you completed each day.

Date:

Habits Practised Today	Response
Comfortable Eating	
Eating on Schedule prepared	
Daily Exercise	
6-8 Hours of Sleep	
Silence Moment	

🎯 Practice 3: Reflection at the End of the Week

After 7 days, answer these questions in your notebook

- What small change made the biggest difference in how I feel?
- Did I ignore or delay anything my body was asking for? Why?
- How can I be more kind and caring to my body next week?

Date:

Weekly Review	Response
Biggest Change Impact	
Ignored Body Signals?	
Body kindness plan?	

🎯 Practice 4: Reminder Affirmation (Say this daily):

"I listen to my body. I respect its needs. I care for it with love."

Notes

Chapter 3

The Whisper of Knowledge

In the previous chapter, we explored the benefits of being healthy and learned how to create a "Health Atom." Now, we will shift our focus to another equally vital element that is essential for building our inner fusion.

Knowledge is everything we know and understand. It includes the facts we read in books, the information we gather from the world, the skills we pick up through practice, and the wisdom we gain through life itself. Knowledge is not just something stored in the brain instead, it's something that shapes the way we think, the choices we make, and the way we live each day.

It grows quietly and continuously. Every time we observe something new, reflect on an idea, have a conversation, or learn from another person, we are adding a new piece to our collection of knowledge. Simply put, knowledge helps us make sense of the world around us. Without it, life would feel like wandering in darkness. With it, we find direction, meaning, and the ability to move forward.

Each person has their own unique understanding of life. No two people, not even twins, know the exact same things in the exact same way. Our minds are like gardens in which what grows in them depends on the seeds planted, the care given, and the environment surrounding them.

Let's take an example. Imagine two best friends. They went to the same school, studied in the same college, and now even work in the same company, doing the same job. On the surface, it may look like their knowledge is identical. After all, they attended the same classes, read the same textbooks, and shared many experiences together.

But if we look closer, their inner worlds are not the same. Why?

Because they come from different families, were raised with different values, have different beliefs, and faced different situations in life. One may have grown up in a strict household that taught discipline above all, while the other may have been raised in a family that encouraged creativity and freedom. One may have faced financial struggles early in life, while the other may never have worried about money. These differences leave deep marks, shaping how each of them thinks, reacts, and learns.

Even though they spent years side by side, their personal knowledge is unique. And that's the beauty of being human. Each of us carries our own world of experiences, insights, and lessons.

Now, let's take this one step further. If we all carry our own special knowledge, then it's worth asking: *What are the things everyone should know to grow and glow as a person?*

By "glow," we don't mean shiny clothes or bright lights. We mean the glow that shows on your face when you are happy, peaceful, and confident from within. It is the glow of someone who is in balance with life, who has both wisdom and warmth.

The wonderful thing about knowledge is that it never truly ends. It grows with us. A child knows the world differently from a teenager. An adult sees things differently from a grandparent. At every stage of life, we discover new truths.

Sometimes, knowledge comes from books and formal education. Other times, it comes from a mistake we made, a conversation with a stranger, or a quiet moment of reflection. Even failure, if looked at carefully, can give us valuable knowledge that success cannot.

That's why it's said that *Knowledge is power.* But it's more than just power, it is also light. It shows us where we are going. It helps us grow not just smarter, but wiser.

Knowledge is not one-size-fits-all. It is as unique as our fingerprints, shaped by where we come from, what we go through, and how we choose to learn. And while each of us carries different knowledge, there are certain essentials about health, relationships, self, the world, and balance that help every person grow and glow from within.

So, as we continue our journey through life, the question to carry with us is simple: *What am I learning today that will help me live a better tomorrow?* Because the truth is, every bit of knowledge we gather is like a small lamp. Alone, it may light only a little space. But together, all our lamps create the glow that makes life truly meaningful.

So, what kind of knowledge helps us reach that state?

Your Personal Defence System

You might have heard in the news about defence systems, especially during recent tensions between India and Pakistan in May 2025. The country's defence system protected our borders by stopping enemy missiles and drones. It was strong, smart, and ready.

But here's an important question:

Do you have a defence system for your own mind and heart?

In daily life, we often get hurt not by missiles but by words, actions, and emotions.

- Someone might say something that hurts your feelings.
- A comment may lower your confidence.
- People sometimes pass on their own stress or negativity to you, leaving you upset.

So, just like a country protects itself from outside attacks, you need to protect yourself from emotional and mental attacks. That's where your personal defence system comes in.

Let me share something personal. I've built my own inner defence system, and I've given it a name, Pluto.

When I was a child, I learned that there were nine planets in our solar system, and Pluto was the ninth. But years later, scientists decided Pluto is not a planet anymore. They said there are only eight.

Now here's the interesting part about Pluto. It doesn't care what scientists think about it. It doesn't matter to Pluto whether it's considered part of the solar system or not. Pluto didn't change its path. It didn't stop spinning or moving. It just kept going. Quietly. Happily. Being itself.

That's the kind of strength we all need.

Be like Pluto:

- Keep going, even if people say you don't fit.
- Walk your own path, even if others don't understand.
- Find joy in your journey, even if others don't approve.
- Know your own worth, no matter what labels others give you.

Pluto reminds us that self-belief is the best protection. Build your own Pluto Defence System.

Respect And Self - Respect

One of the most important values we must carry through life is respect both for others and for ourselves.

We meet all kinds of people: friends, family, colleagues, teachers, and even strangers. No matter who they are, the least we can offer them is basic respect.

That means:

- Speak kindly.
- Listen without judging.
- Avoid insults or harsh words.

- Stay calm even during disagreements.

Yes, disagreements will happen. That's normal. But disagreeing doesn't mean we have to shout, insult, or hurt someone. We can express our thoughts clearly and calmly, without causing pain.

I once worked in a company where seniors often humiliated a few of their team members. People were spoken to rudely, sometimes even in front of others. These employees felt small and powerless. Their self-respect was slowly breaking.

It was a toxic environment, and it hurt even if you were not part of it.

That's when I understood something clearly. Just like we should respect others, we must also demand respect for ourselves.

If someone treats you badly or disrespects you, it is your responsibility to protect your self-respect. But do it wisely.

Don't fight with anger. Don't return insult for insult. Just stand firm, stay calm, and let your actions and presence send a clear message:

"I will not let anyone break my dignity."

Believe In Yourself

Believing in yourself is more than just a nice thought—it's one of the most important things you can do for your growth and success in life. It means trusting your abilities, having faith in your choices, and knowing that you can handle challenges, even when things get tough or others doubt you.

Many people, including some of my friends, have said that it's hard to stay confident during hard times. And they're right. When things don't go as planned, it's natural to feel confused, sad, or unsure of yourself. But this is exactly when believing in yourself becomes truly important.

Believing in yourself during good times is easy. The real test is when life gets difficult. It doesn't mean ignoring your problems or pretending everything is okay. It means staying calm, not blaming yourself or others, and reminding yourself that tough times don't last forever. It's about saying to yourself, "Yes, this is hard, but I can get through it."

Think of life like sailing a boat. When the sea is calm, anyone can steer. But when a storm comes, your belief in your ability to keep going becomes your guide. It helps you stay strong and find your way, even when you can't see the shore.

When you believe in yourself, you are more likely to take chances, face your fears, and learn from mistakes. This kind of belief helps you keep moving forward, no matter how slow the progress is. Over time, it becomes a part of who you are, a strong mindset that helps you in every situation.

Even during difficult times, believing in yourself means living fully, not giving up, and being your own biggest supporter. And when you do this, you can also inspire the people around you.

So next time you hear someone say "Believe in yourself," remember that it's not about being perfect. It's about trusting that you have what it takes to handle whatever comes your way. The road may not be easy, but your belief in yourself will help you walk it with courage and hope.

Because in the end, believing in yourself is one of the best gifts you can give to yourself and to the world.

Whenever you feel low, just remember what Lord Krishna told Arjuna in the Mahabharata. It's written in The Bhagavad Gita. The Gita is not just for religious people. It's a guide for anyone who wants to live wisely, bravely, and peacefully.

The Gita teaches that life is full of challenges, but if we do our duties with the right attitude and keep faith, we can live a peaceful and meaningful life.

Life Lessons from Gita:

- **Do your duty** without worrying about the results.
- **Work honestly and selflessly**, without being greedy or selfish.
- **Love and trust God**, and stay connected with him through devotion.
- **Understand your true self**; you are not just your body, but an eternal soul.
- **Stay calm** in good and bad times, and keep your mind balanced.

Work Life Balance

Work-life balance means managing your job and personal life in a way that neither one suffers. It's about giving time to your work responsibilities while also taking care of your health, family, relationships, and personal interests. In today's life, offices are often far from home, and heavy traffic causes more delays. Because of this, it's becoming hard to find enough time for personal life. On top of that, in many jobs, people have to work longer hours than what is officially required.

Just like we discussed earlier about improving your health by taking small, manageable steps, the same approach works for managing your time better. It's important to start with very small changes. At the beginning, you might feel like nothing is changing or improving, and that's okay. Change often takes time. But if you keep practising these small steps consistently, over time you will definitely notice a positive difference. This improvement will show not only in how your day goes but also in your mood, you'll feel happier, more relaxed, and more confident.

I have seen many people work hard to improve their work-life balance, and they have been successful in making more time for their family. That's a wonderful achievement. But sometimes, in the process, they forget about the most important person in their life, "themselves". Work-life balance is not just about dividing your time between work and family. It's about balancing three important parts: your work, your family, and *you*.

You are the centre of this balance because, without taking care of yourself, you won't have the energy, focus, or happiness to give your best at work or be fully present with your family. Self-care is not selfish; it's necessary. If you don't make time for yourself, your time spent with your family or at work won't be as meaningful or productive as it could be.

Think about the safety instructions you hear on aeroplanes saying that if the oxygen level drops, you are told to put on your own oxygen mask first before helping others. This advice is important because you need to be strong and well before you can support anyone else.

The same idea applies to everyday life. Taking time for yourself should be your priority. When you do this, you recharge your mind and body. Then, you can give your best to your family and your work. That's how you create true balance, a balance where all three parts support and strengthen each other.

Remember, small steps in managing your time and prioritising yourself will gradually lead to a happier, healthier, and more fulfilling life for you and everyone around you.

Work is important, but so is living a happy, peaceful, and meaningful life. A good work-life balance leads to better well-being and long-term success.

When you bring your qualities, i.e. self-respect, belief, strength, and confidence together inside you, you create your own kind of energy. This energy will light up your life. It will give you the strength to face challenges, the courage to follow your dreams, and the calm to stay happy, even in difficult times.

You might think, “This sounds good, but I’m not a leader or a public speaker. I’m just a regular person.”

It does not matter what your job or role is. These qualities are for everyone to like.

- An engineer, solving problems with machines,
- A doctor, helping people heal,
- A lawyer, fighting for justice,
- Or even a homemaker, taking care of your family and managing your home with love

No matter who you are or what you do, these qualities will help you shine. When you start building these important life habits, you begin to create what I like to call a “Knowledge Atom.”

Key Takeaways

Build Your Own Personal Defence System – equipping yourself with inner strength and strategies to face any challenge life throws your way.

Honour Your True Self – setting boundaries, valuing who you are, and never settling for less than you deserve

Unshakeable Self - Belief – trusting your abilities even when the world doubts you

Mastering Work Life Harmony – creating a lifestyle where career growth and personal joy go hand in hand

Miracle of cultivating a 'Knowledge Atom'– fueling your mind with insights that lead to innovation and transformation

Practice Exercise

Build Your Inner Shield: *Practical Exercises to Strengthen Your Inner World and Balance Your Outer Life*

🎯 Practice 1: Building Your Personal Defence System

"Not everything deserves a reaction. Build boundaries, not walls."

☞ Exercise 1: Energy Audit

- List 5 situations that drained your energy last week.
- Write what you could have done to protect your peace.
- What kind of boundaries (time, emotional, digital) can you set starting today?

📝 ***Write your answers in a small notebook.***

Date:

Energy drain list
How to Protect my peace?
Boundary setting plan

☞ Exercise 2: Mental Armour Checklist

Daily checklist:

Date:

Action Item	Response
I paused before reacting	
I said "no" without guilt	
I protected my focus time	
I disconnected from toxic inputs (social media, gossip, etc.)	

🎯 Practice 2: Cultivating Self-Respect

"You teach others how to treat you by how you treat yourself."

☞ Exercise 1: Respect Reflection

Date:

Action Item	Response
List five actions or habits where you disrespect yourself (e.g., overcommitting, negative self-talk).	
Write one way to reverse each habit.	

☞ Exercise 2: Your Non-Negotiables

Create a list of your top five values. For each value, write one personal boundary that supports it.

Date:

Value System	Personal Boundary

Example: Value: Health → Boundary: I won't work past 8 PM without dinner and a walk.

Practice 3: Believing In Yourself

"You've Survived 100% of your worst days. That's proof enough."

☞ Exercise 1: Rewriting the Inner Voice

- Write three common negative thoughts you have about yourself.
- Replace each with a powerful belief.
- Repeat the new belief every morning for a week.

Date:

Negative Thoughts	Powerful Belief

☞ Exercise 2: I Am Proof Journal

Date:

Experience	Outcome
Write about one past experience where you overcame fear or failure.	
What strengths did you use?	
What does that prove about who you are?	

🎯 Practice 4: Work-Life Balance Reset

"Balance isn't about equal time—it's about aligned priorities."

☞ Exercise 1: Time Mapping

Track how you spent your last 3 days (hour by hour).

Date:

Experience	Outcome
Work, Family, Self-Care, Distraction, anything else	
What patterns do you notice?	
Where can you reduce or realign time?	

☞ Exercise 2: Balance It Out

Create a chart divided into 6 parts:

Time Chart	Rating
Work	
Family	
Health	
Friends	
Hobbies	
Rest	

Rate each from 1–10

- Which area needs the most attention?
- Write one small improvement you'll take this week.

Notes

Chapter 4

A Silent Revolution

In the earlier chapters, we discussed the importance of creating both the Health Atom and the Knowledge Atom. Now, we turn to the final aspect that is essential for generating inner fusion.

This chapter is about you. Not your job, not your responsibilities, not your relationships, but the real *you* at the core of everything. You have the power to create wonders. You carry within you the calmness that can bring peace, clarity, strength, and direction.

It is very important for every individual to remain calm from within. Inner calmness helps us think clearly, act wisely, and live peacefully. But a common question that comes to mind is whether there is a fixed or defined method to achieve this calmness? The honest answer is no. There is no single formula or a rulebook to find inner peace.

However, there are many practices and habits that, when followed regularly and sincerely, can lead you toward a deeper connection with yourself and even with the divine. These practices help you slow down, go inward, and touch a space where there is no noise, no chaos, and no confusion. Only peace, silence, and stillness.

You may find this connection through meditation, letting go, having a purpose in life, stop procrastinating, celebrating or even through simple acts of kindness and gratitude. Everyone's path is different. What matters is consistency and a genuine intention to connect with your inner self.

When you make time for such activities, day after day, you will start to notice a change not outside, but inside. Your reactions soften, your mind quiets down, your stress begins to melt, and in its place, a quiet strength begins to grow. This is the calmness that doesn't depend on the world being perfect. It comes from within.

So, while there is no fixed road, there is a direction that leads inward. Walk it with faith, and you'll find what you're looking for not outside, but within your own soul.

Meditation

It's a tool to connect with your thoughts, feelings, and breath. It helps you slow down the noise of the outside world and listen to your inner voice. When practised regularly, meditation becomes a habit that brings calm even in the middle of chaos. Meditation is not just about sitting quietly with your eyes closed. It's a simple practice that helps you calm your mind and feel more peaceful. There are many different ways to meditate, and each person can choose what works best for them.

Some common types of meditation include:

- Breathing Meditation – focusing on your breath to relax your mind.

- Mantra Chanting – repeating a word or phrase to help you stay focused.
- Body Scan Meditation – paying attention to different parts of your body to release stress.
- Visualisation – imagining a calm place like a beach or forest to feel peaceful.

There is no "one perfect way" that works for everyone. You can try different methods and see which one makes you feel better.

The main goal of meditation is to help you:

- Reduce stress and tension
- Improve focus and concentration
- Think more clearly
- Feel more creative
- Stay positive and calm

Besides these benefits, meditation also improves your health, like better sleep, lower blood pressure, and stronger immunity. It also helps you connect with yourself on a deeper level and can bring a sense of spiritual peace.

While practising daily meditation, your mind may sometimes tell you it's a waste of time or that it doesn't work. For some, the benefits appear quickly, while for many, it takes longer. Be patient and continue the practice, even if it feels like it isn't helping right away. The key is to practice regularly, even for a few minutes each day. With time, you'll notice how much more peaceful and balanced you feel both in your mind and in your daily life.

A Journey Within

Riya was a young professional working in a fast-paced city. Her days began with endless notifications, back-to-back meetings, and the constant pressure to perform. By the time she returned home, her mind was still racing with unfinished tasks and future worries. Sleep never came easily, and peace always felt far away.

One evening, while scrolling through social media, Riya came across a short video on meditation. It spoke about slowing down and connecting with your breath. Sceptical but curious, she decided to give it a try. She sat on her bed, closed her eyes, and focused on her breathing. Within a minute, her thoughts began to wander: *"This is useless. I can't sit still. I have so much to do."* She opened her eyes, frustrated.

But something inside nudged her to try again the next morning. This time, she set a timer for just two minutes and promised herself she wouldn't judge the experience. Slowly, she noticed her breath flowing in and out. For the first time in days, her mind felt a little lighter.

Encouraged, Riya began exploring different types of meditation. On some days, she practised **breathing meditation**, simply noticing her inhale and exhale. On other days, she tried **mantra chanting**, softly repeating a phrase that kept her centred. She even discovered **visualisation**, imagining herself sitting by the ocean, listening to the waves. Each method gave her a new way to find peace.

At first, the changes were subtle. She still had deadlines and challenges, but her reactions were calmer. She no longer snapped at her colleagues. She began sleeping better. Even her creativity at work improved, as if her mind had been cleared of unnecessary clutter.

Weeks turned into months, and meditation became a trusted companion. Riya realised it wasn't about sitting perfectly still or emptying the mind. It was about building a quiet space within, where she could return anytime life felt overwhelming.

Through meditation, she learned three important truths:

1. Peace doesn't come from controlling the outside world instead, it begins within.
2. A few minutes of stillness each day can transform the way you face challenges.
3. Patience and consistency are the keys to unlocking the deeper benefits of meditation.

Today, Riya continues her practice daily. Sometimes it's five minutes, sometimes twenty. No matter how busy life gets, she knows that meditation is not an escape, but it's her way of connecting with herself, reducing stress, and staying grounded in a noisy world.

And just like Riya, anyone can begin this journey. All it takes is a moment, a breath, and the willingness to listen to the silence within.

Letting Go

"Letting go" is one of the easiest things to say to others, but often the hardest thing to do for ourselves. Why? Because from a young age, many of us are conditioned to hold on to guilt, past mistakes, regrets, and even grudges. These emotional burdens stay with us for years, sometimes even a lifetime, causing pain and limiting our happiness.

But is there truly no way to let go of all this? The answer is Yes; there is a way. And it begins by understanding one important thing: most of these heavy emotions come from fear.

- Fear of accepting our mistakes, so we live with guilt.
- Fear of speaking up when something feels wrong, so we carry grudges.
- Fear of failure, so we avoid risks and stay stuck in the past.

If you can let go of just "fear", you'll find it much easier to let go of everything else. Letting go of fear gives you the strength to:

- Accept your faults and grow from them.
- Speak up respectfully when something bothers you.
- Take action even when you're unsure of the result.
- Move forward, even if you've failed before.

ANGER
HATE
HATE
FEAR
REGRET
PAIN

But this doesn't happen overnight. It takes practice, patience, and small, brave steps every time you face a difficult moment. For example:

- Speak your truth kindly, even if it's uncomfortable.
- Say "no" when something doesn't feel right.
- Try again, even if you failed last time.
- Tell someone calmly that their words or actions hurt you.

The more you practice, the stronger you become. With time, you'll notice something powerful, and you're no longer carrying the same guilt, pain, or resentment. You'll feel lighter.

You'll feel free. You'll feel more like your true self without fear, without grudges, and without regret.

The Balloon

In a small town nestled between the hills, lived an old man named Kabir. Every evening, he sat on a bench near the lake, watching the sky turn golden. Beside him, he always carried a small red balloon—worn, deflated, yet carefully tied to a string.

People often wondered why an old man would carry such a thing. Some thought it was a memory, others thought it was a message. But no one asked. Until one day, a curious little boy named Aarav walked up and asked, "Uncle, why do you carry that balloon every day?"

Kabir smiled, eyes softening.

"This balloon," he said, "was a gift from my daughter. On her fifth birthday, she gave it to me and said, 'Now you have something to hold when I'm not around.' A few years later, she passed away in an accident."

Aarav's smile faded. "I'm sorry…"

Kabir nodded. "For years, I held onto it like it was the last piece of her. I couldn't let go. I thought if I did, I'd be letting go of her."

"But today," Kabir said, "something feels different. I've come to understand that she's not in this balloon. She's in my memories. She's in my smile. She's in the breeze that touches my face when I miss her."

With trembling hands, he untied the string. The old red balloon, though barely filled, caught the light breeze and floated upward.

Kabir and Aarav watched in silence.

"Letting go," Kabir said gently, "doesn't mean forgetting. It means making space for peace."

Letting go isn't about losing. It's about freeing yourself to heal, to breathe, and to love again with an open heart.

Purpose of Life

Calmness begins when you understand your "why?"

Why do you get out of bed every morning?

What makes you feel excited, happy, or alive?

What is that one thing you wish to share with the world?

Your "why" is your purpose because of which you do what you do. It doesn't need to be big or fancy. It can be something simple and beautiful, like:

- Helping others in need
- Making someone smile
- Teaching what you know
- Creating something meaningful
- Taking care of your family
- Becoming a better version of yourself each day

Having a purpose gives you a clear direction in life. It makes your efforts feel valuable. Even when life gets tough, your purpose reminds you that there's a reason to keep going.

Calmness grows stronger when life feels meaningful. And meaning doesn't come only from big success or awards. It comes from:

- Small acts of kindness
- Learning something new
- Being useful to others
- Taking care of yourself
- Doing things with love and attention
- Growing slowly, one step at a time

When your life has meaning you feel more stable and peaceful inside.

You stop feeling lost. You stop chasing things that don't matter. You feel more focused, more content, and more grounded even during difficult times. That is the power of knowing your purpose. It brings clarity, peace, and strength, and helps you stay calm no matter what comes your way. Just create a purpose in life and live on that.

Once you start meditating and let go of things that don't matter, you will slowly begin to discover your true purpose in life.

The Story of Arjun Finding Purpose

Arjun was living what most people would call a "successful life." He had a good job, a nice apartment, and a stable income. Yet every morning when the alarm rang, he felt a strange emptiness. He asked himself, *"Why am I even doing this? What's the point?"*

The days went by in a blur of deadlines, meetings, and endless scrolling on his phone. At night, when he lay in bed, his mind was restless. He wondered if life was only about earning, eating, and sleeping. Deep down, he knew something was missing.

One Sunday morning, while sitting quietly in a park, Arjun noticed an old man feeding stray dogs. The man smiled at each dog as if it were his own. Curious, Arjun asked, "Why do you do this every day?"

The old man replied gently, "Because it makes me happy to give. This is my purpose, which gives me peace."

Those simple words struck Arjun deeply. For the first time, he realised that purpose didn't have to be something grand like becoming famous or changing the world. It could be something small yet powerful that made life feel meaningful.

That evening, Arjun began reflecting on his own life. Slowly, he discovered his "why." Arjun loved teaching. He remembered how alive he felt when he helped his younger cousin with studies, and how his colleagues often came to him for guidance. So, he decided to spend a few hours each week mentoring children in his neighbourhood who couldn't afford tuition.

At first, it was just two kids. Then, more joined. With every lesson, Arjun felt lighter, calmer, and more joyful. Work stress still existed, but it no longer consumed him. His purpose gave him a reason to get up in the morning, and even on tough days, it reminded him that his life mattered.

Through this journey, Arjun realised a profound truth that purpose isn't always found in big achievements, instead it is created in small acts of love, kindness, and growth. When life has purpose, calmness follows naturally.

Today, Arjun continues his job, but with new energy. He knows his life is not just about earning; it's about sharing, growing, and giving. His purpose keeps him grounded, peaceful, and fulfilled.

And just like Arjun, each of us has a "why" waiting to be discovered. It may be hidden in something simple like helping, creating, caring, or learning. Once you find it, life stops feeling like a race and starts feeling like a journey worth living.

Procrastination

Procrastination means delaying or avoiding tasks, even when we know they are important. It usually happens when we feel lazy, scared to fail, confused, or don't know where to begin. At first, it may feel okay to delay things, but later it causes stress, pressure, and regret. The longer we wait, the harder it gets to start. The best way to beat procrastination is to start small. Do one simple thing first. Break big tasks into small steps and feel good after finishing each part. What matters is moving forward—not being perfect. When you take small steps every day, you feel more confident and get things done on time.

Procrastination can be considered like a true friend, one that lives inside each of us. But this friend often holds us back. Whenever we want to try something new or different, it shows up and fills our minds with doubts, fears, and what might go wrong. Instead of giving us courage, it makes us feel weaker and stops us from taking action.

The good news is, you can overcome this so-called friend. All it takes is the courage to take small, bold steps even when you feel afraid. At first, it may be difficult, but with time and effort, procrastination will slowly lose its power. One day, you'll notice that it no longer controls you, and you'll feel free to act on your goals with confidence.

PROCRASTINATION

The Story of Aarav and His Silent Friend

Aarav had always dreamed of starting his own blog. He loved writing and wanted to share his thoughts with the world. But every evening, when he sat down to write, something strange happened. A little voice in his head whispered, *"You're too tired. Do it tomorrow. What if no one likes what you write? Maybe you're not good enough."*

That voice felt like a friend who cared, convincing him to rest or "wait for the right time." Aarav listened, thinking he was being wise. Days turned into weeks, and weeks into months. His blog remained a blank page.

At first, he told himself it didn't matter. But slowly, he began to feel restless. He saw others chasing their dreams, while he was stuck. One day, Aarav met his mentor, who asked enquired that why he hadn't started his blog yet.

Aarav sighed. "I don't know where to begin. And I'm afraid it won't be perfect." His mentor smiled and replied, "Perfection is a trap. Start small. Write one sentence today. Tomorrow, write a paragraph. Break it down into steps. Progress, not perfection, is what matters."

That evening, Aarav sat at his desk again. The little voice his silent friend, Procrastination appeared once again saying *"You can do it tomorrow."*

But this time, Aarav smiled back. He wrote just one sentence. The next day, he wrote a little more. Within a week, he had his first blog post ready. It wasn't perfect, but it was real. And it was his.

Slowly, Aarav discovered that every small step weakened the grip of procrastination. The more he acted, the quieter that voice became. One day, he realised something powerful that procrastination had never been a true friend instead, it was only fear in disguise.

From then on, Aarav carried a new belief to start small, take one step at a time and keep moving forward. And with every step, he built not only his blog, but also his confidence and freedom.

Celebrating

Sometimes, we are so busy thinking about the next thing we need to do that we forget to look back and see how much we've already done. True calmness grows when you pause and appreciate your journey. It's not just about big achievements or winning awards, it's also about the small moments when you choose to be kind, honest, patient, or brave.

You've grown more than you realise. You've faced challenges, learned new things, and kept going even when it was hard. That deserves to be celebrated. You should be thankful for every positive thing that happens in your life.

Life is not only about reaching big goals. It's also about enjoying the little things. Celebrate your mornings. Celebrate the food you eat. Celebrate your small wins, your friendships, your efforts. Laugh when you can. Dance when you feel happy. Smile even on an ordinary day.

Don't wait for something huge to happen to feel joy. Start enjoying life today, just as it is. A heart that celebrates often is a heart that feels calm, happy, and at peace.

The Story of Meera's Little Celebrations

Meera was always chasing the next milestone. At work, she wanted the next promotion. At home, she wanted the next big purchase. Even in her personal goals, she kept telling herself, *"I'll be happy when..."*

But no matter what she achieved, the happiness was short-lived. The next day, a new target would take its place. Deep down, Meera felt tired and wondered why peace seemed so far away.

One evening, after a particularly hectic day, she sat on her balcony with a cup of tea. She noticed the sky slowly changing colours as the sun set. For the first time in weeks, she paused and simply watched. A gentle smile crossed her face. It felt… calming.

The next morning, instead of rushing straight into emails, Meera wrote down three things she was grateful for: her health, a supportive friend who had called her the previous night and the warm cup of tea that gave her comfort. That small act felt surprisingly joyful. Over the next few days, she began noticing little things worth celebrating. This can be

- Finishing a report on time.
- Cooking a simple but tasty meal.
- Helping a colleague who was struggling.
- Laughing with her neighbour's child.

These moments weren't big, but they filled her heart with lightness. She realised that celebration wasn't only for birthdays, promotions, or awards. Actually, it was for the little victories and blessings that made life meaningful.

Slowly, Meera's perspective shifted. Instead of waiting for "someday," she began celebrating "today." A smile became her celebration. A quiet walk became her celebration. A good conversation became her celebration.

Through this, she discovered a new truth that **celebration is not about what you achieve, but it's about how you choose to live each moment.**

Meera didn't stop working toward her goals, but she no longer tied her happiness to them. Her calmness grew naturally because her heart had learned the secret of joy by appreciating the journey, one small celebration at a time.

Calmness Atom

As you begin to focus on practices like meditation, letting go, discovering your life's purpose, overcoming procrastination, and celebrating small wins, you will gradually create a unique inner energy within yourself, which I call the **"Calmness Atom."**

Just like every physical atom is made up of smaller parts like protons, neutrons, and electrons, the Calmness Atom is made up of powerful elements of the mind and spirit that together create stability, strength, and peace.

Key Takeaways

Embrace the Power of Meditation – create inner stillness and build a daily practice that nourishes your mind, body, and soul.

Learn the Art of Letting Go – free yourself from the weight of the past and open space for peace and new possibilities.

Discover Your True - Life Purpose – explore what truly matters to you and align your actions with a deeper meaning.

Break Free from Procrastination – replace delays with discipline and move confidently toward your goals.

Celebrate Every Win, Big or Small – cultivate joy and gratitude by honouring your progress at every step.

Unlock Your 'Calmness Atom' – tap into your inner reservoir of peace and carry it into everything you do.

Practice Exercise

Inner Clarity and Growth

1. MEDITATION – Anchoring the Mind

☞ Exercise: Three Minute Breath Awareness

- Sit comfortably.
- Close your eyes and focus on your breath.
- Inhale: Say "I am here."
- Exhale: Say "I am calm."
- Continue for 3 minutes.
- Journal: What thoughts distracted you? What did you feel?

Do this before major decisions or stressful moments.

2. LETTING GO – Releasing What No Longer Serves

☞ Exercise: Release & Replace

Write down 3 things/people/situations you are holding onto emotionally. Write down what fear or belief keeps you attached?	
1	
2	
Now write what you are ready to replace them with: e.g., Let go of perfection → Embrace progress.	
1	
2	

Imagine these worries as leaves floating down a river. Watch them drift away. Breathe deeply.

3. PURPOSE OF LIFE – Connecting to Your Why

☞ Exercise 1: Life Lens Journal

Answer the following:

Action Item	Response
What makes me feel alive?	
What problems in the world make me want to help?	
If I had no fear or limitations, what would I do?	
Who benefits when I'm at my best?	

☞ Exercise 2: Purpose Prompt

Finish this sentence and read this daily:

"My life matters because..."

4. PROCRASTINATION – Taking the First Step

Practice: Five Minute Push

- Pick one task you've been avoiding.
- Set a timer for just five minutes.
- Start without pressure to finish it.
- At the end, five minutes:

How did you start feeling?

What did you notice about your resistance?

You need to understand that you do not need to be great to start. You need to start being great. Small starts beat big intentions.

5. CELEBRATING – Honouring Small Wins

🎯 Practice: Daily Brag Sheet

At the end of each day, write:

Action Item	Response
One thing I did well today	
One effort I'm proud of (even if the result was small)	
One way I showed up for myself	

Treat yourself for consistency, not just success. Celebration builds self-respect.

This is a moment to pause and reflect. Why did we begin reading this book? What are we truly hoping to gain from it?

Now that we've understood the basic ideas needed to build our personal fusion reaction, it's time to move ahead. The next step is to reconnect with the inner glow we may have lost over time. A glow that comes from true happiness, kindness, confidence, and a life free from regret.

In the coming chapters, we'll explore a few more basics. After that, we'll dive into something many of you have been waiting for.

Notes

PART - 2

BUILDING YOUR PERSONAL FUSION

Chapter 5

What It Matters to You?

In the noise of everyday life, it's easy to lose sight of what truly matters. We chase deadlines, fulfil responsibilities, and go through routines often without pausing to ask ourselves one simple yet powerful question.

"What really matters to me?"

This question is not just about goals or desires. It's about values. It's about alignment. It's about living a life that reflects your inner truth, not someone else's expectations.

When you know what matters to you, your life gains direction. Choices become clearer. Decisions become easier. You stop getting lost in distractions and start living with purpose.

Sometimes we forget what matters because we've been too busy surviving. Surviving becomes such a priority that we forget other aspects of life and put our entire focus on surviving as if we lose control this, we will lose life. Sometimes we compromise bit by bit until we're no longer sure what we stand for. And sometimes we simply never ask ourselves the question in the first place.

Sometimes, in the rush of daily life, we forget what truly matters. We become so busy **just surviving**, meeting deadlines, paying bills, handling responsibilities that survival itself begins to feel like our only purpose.

SURVIVAL
PURPOSE

It takes up all our focus, as if losing control over it would mean losing life itself.

In this process, we often begin to **compromise little by little**. We set aside our passions, silence our inner voice, and ignore the values we once believed in. Slowly, almost without noticing, we find ourselves uncertain of what we truly stand for.

And sometimes, the reason is even simpler than we never really paused to ask ourselves the deeper questions:

- *What do I value most?*
- *What gives my life meaning beyond survival?*
- *Who am I when the noise of the world is silent?*

Without reflection, we risk living on autopilot, where days pass but fulfilment feels absent.

Knowing what matters is only the beginning. The real transformation happens when you begin to **live** by it consciously, consistently, and courageously. When we take the first step from mere survival toward **living with purpose, clarity, and calmness**.

What truly matters to you could be the key to your life's purpose. Once you understand and connect with that purpose, you naturally start focusing on the things that really count. You stop wasting time on things that don't matter. You begin to say a clear 'no' to distractions. You don't need to follow someone else's path. You have your own direction, which is your own inner compass. That compass is made from your values, dreams, and what's important to you. Keep it close and trust it. The journey might not always be smooth, but it will be yours. And that makes every step worth it

The Lamp and The Wind

Once, there was a small oil lamp placed on a windowsill. Every night, it would light up the room with its gentle glow. One stormy evening, strong winds howled outside. The lamp began to flicker and thought, *"What's the point of trying to shine in such a storm? The darkness is too strong."*

Just then, an old traveller entered the room, cold and tired. Seeing the faint light, he smiled and said, *"Ah, this little flame guided me home."*

The lamp suddenly understood that its purpose wasn't to fight the whole darkness but just to light up the space around it. That was enough.

If someone asks me what my purpose in life is, I would say **"to spread happiness."**

I feel happy when I see the people around me smiling and at peace. If someone close to me is feeling low, I try my best to cheer them up. I do whatever I can, with all my effort and love, to bring back their smile. Even if I can't solve their problems, I make sure they don't feel alone. I stay by their side during tough times. Helping others feel better gives me a sense of joy and makes me feel complete.

So, if you want to find purpose in your life, ask yourself what matters to you most. Is it

- Peace, Growth, connection, freedom, integrity or something else?
- What kind of experiences make you feel most alive?

- When do you feel most like yourself?
- Who or what are you willing to stand up for, even when it's hard?

Write down your answers. Reflect on them. They are not just thoughts; they are signposts pointing to your personal truth.

It's never too late to reconnect. Go back to your childhood. What brought you joy? What made you feel safe? What did you dream of?

Revisit your hard times. What kept you going? What gave you strength? Often, what matters most to us hides quietly in the stories of both joy and pain.

Once you know what you need to work on, **don't wait; start right away**. Take the first step as soon as you realise what needs to be done.

There's a powerful saying: **"You don't have to be good to start, but you have to start to become good."**

So don't wait for the perfect moment. Don't worry about what others will think. Don't wait until you feel fully ready. Don't stay silent when you have something to say. Don't keep saying "yes" to things that don't bring you joy or meaning.

Start with small steps. Even tiny actions matter. These little steps will slowly build your confidence, remove self-doubt, and fill you with happiness. Over time, they will lead you toward the success and peace you're looking for.

The journey begins the moment you start. So, take that first step now.

Key Takeaways

Ask Yourself What Truly Matters – your values, not just your goals, define your direction.

Live by Your Inner Compass – let your values, dreams, and truth guide every choice.

Purpose is Personal – you don't need to fight the whole darkness, just light your own space.

Stand Up for What You Believe – even when it's hard, your courage shapes your purpose.

Start Before You Feel Ready – small steps today create big transformations tomorrow.

Say 'No' to Distractions – free your time and energy for what brings real meaning.

Consistency is Power – transformation comes from living your truth every day, not just realising it once.

Notes

Chapter 6

Healing And Emotional Release

Whatever we hear, see, or experience, our mind immediately starts giving it a meaning. Mind connects words and situations with our past experiences. It creates different possibilities, even when nothing is clearly said. It is also said that the mind is a meaning-making machine. The moment you give it a thought to process, it starts creating multiple interpretations.

This happens because of the way our mind has been shaped over time. It is influenced by our old beliefs, our ego, our fears, and the assumptions we've made throughout life. So sometimes, the meaning we create may not be true. It's just how our mind is trying to protect us or make sense of things based on our past. To really understand things clearly, we need to be aware of this habit and sometimes pause and ask ourselves

"Is this what's really happening, or just what my mind is making it mean?"

The Music of the Flute

There was once a wise musician who played the most beautiful melodies on a simple bamboo flute. One day, a curious traveller asked him, "How does such a hollow stick make such soulful music?"

The musician smiled and said, "Because it is empty inside."

He continued, "The bamboo had to let go of everything i.e. its core, its knots, its pride of being strong, to become this flute. Only by becoming empty could it carry the wind and create music that touches hearts."

The traveller stood in silence, deeply moved. He realised that sometimes, to be useful, peaceful, or creative, we must let go of our inner noise and make space within.

Emptying yourself doesn't mean losing who you are. It means leaving what no longer serves you, like stress, ego, fear, and mental clutter. With this, you can feel lighter, clearer, and more at peace.

If you too wish to feel lighter, calmer, and more at peace, you can begin by practising a few simple yet powerful habits. These practices, when done consistently, act like gentle tools that clear the clutter of the mind, ease the weight of stress, and create space for inner calm to grow.

1. Breathe

Take a few moments daily to just sit and breathe. No phone, no thoughts to chase—just breathe in and out. This calms your mind and creates space inside you.

❖ Just One Breath

Riya was always in a rush.

Wake up. Check phone. Emails. Coffee. Rush to work. Meetings. Deadlines. Messages. More messages. She lived like she was racing against an invisible clock. Even at night, her mind never slowed down. It was like her life was on fast-forward, and somehow, she was always behind.

One evening, after another exhausting day, she missed her train. Frustrated, she sat on a bench at the quiet station, heart pounding, thoughts spiralling.

"I should've left earlier... Now I'll get home late... So much still to do... I can't keep up..."

As she sat there, an old man on the bench beside her looked over and said kindly, "You're holding your breath."

Riya blinked. "Excuse me?"

He smiled. "You're breathing like the world is chasing you. Try this instead to close your eyes, and just take one deep breath. That's all."

She hesitated. But something in his voice felt safe. She closed her eyes.

Inhale... slowly.

Exhale... deeply.

That one breath felt like a pause in time. The noise in her head softened. Her shoulders dropped.

She opened her eyes.

The train still hadn't come. Her emails were still unanswered. But she felt... different. Still. Present. Alive.

The old man stood up. "Whenever life feels too much, just take one breath. Then take another. Sometimes peace isn't in the solving—it's in the slowing."

He walked away, leaving Riya with something simple but unforgettable.

From that day forward, whenever she felt the world spinning too fast, she remembered: ***Just one breath.*** You don't have to fix everything at once. Sometimes, peace begins with simply remembering to breathe.

2. Observe

Don't believe every thought your mind produces. Just observe them like clouds passing in the sky. You'll start to see which thoughts are just noise and not worth holding onto.

❖ The Sky Within

Ravi sat on the park bench, a cup of tea warming his hands. The day was bright, yet his mind felt overcast. Thoughts swirled in him like restless birds:

"I should've said this... I shouldn't have done that... What if tomorrow goes wrong?"

He closed his eyes. His meditation teacher's words came back to him:

"Don't believe every thought your mind produces. Just observe them, like clouds in the sky."

So, he tried.

One thought came: *"I'm not good enough."* He watched it drift by, a dark little cloud. Another thought: *"I need to do better than everyone else."* That one was jagged, like a storm cloud. And then: *"Maybe I'm okay as I am."* This one felt lighter, like a wisp of white in a blue expanse.

Minutes passed. His thoughts didn't stop, but they slowed, as though embarrassed by the silent witness watching them.

When he opened his eyes, the park looked exactly the same—children still running, leaves still dancing in the breeze. But inside, the sky had cleared.

Not because the clouds were gone, but because he'd finally learned they were just passing through.

3. Detach

You are not just your job, your achievements, or how others see you. These are parts of your life, but they don't define your true worth. When we hold too tightly to our title, image, or the need to always be right, we create pressure and stress for ourselves.

Letting go doesn't mean you stop caring. It means you stop attaching your identity to things that can change, like success, praise, or opinions. You don't have to prove yourself to anyone, all the time. You are enough as you are.

When you stop clinging to your ego, the part of you that always wants to win, to be liked, or to be in control, you feel lighter. You become more open, more relaxed, and more at peace.

Detachment is not disconnection. It's freedom. It allows you to live with confidence, without being ruled by fear, pride, or the need for approval. You're able to focus on what truly matters: inner peace, growth, and meaningful connection.

Nore you! like
Yolly orrelte ymu ko
SHDE IN TOUR MIRIOE
TOAPLE LINE
LAOSYE TIK?
ZZZ
ANAY!
THE COIPPORATIE
SEER STEAR
MANAGER!

❖ The Mirror and the Mask

Anaya was known as "The Star Manager" in her company. Her title was printed in bold on her office door, her achievements framed on the wall, and her phone buzzed constantly with people seeking her approval.

For years, she wore this identity like a jewelled mask, polished, perfect, admired. But one evening, as she was leaving work, she overheard two colleagues say, "If she ever loses this job, I wonder what she'll be without it."

The words stung. She went home and stood in front of her mirror. Without her suit, without the confident tone, without the daily rush—she looked… tired. Who was she when no one was watching?

Over the next weeks, she began a quiet experiment. She stopped introducing herself with her job title. She spent weekends painting, even though she wasn't "good" at it. She learned to enjoy conversations without the need to impress.

It was uncomfortable at first, like walking without armour. But slowly, something shifted. The pressure to prove herself faded. She still cared about her work, but it no longer defined her.

Anaya realised she was more than her role, her wins, or the opinions of others. She was the calm in her own heart, the laughter in her friendships, the joy in doing things just for the sake of doing them.

She hadn't disconnected from life; instead, she'd reconnected with herself. And that was the real freedom.

4. Stop Overthinking

Sometimes our minds go in circles, trying to plan every detail, fix every problem, or predict the future. This constant thinking can leave us feeling tired, anxious, and stuck.

The truth is, you don't need to have all the answers right now. Life doesn't come with a perfect plan, and that's okay. Some things take time to make sense. Some paths only become clear when you start walking.

Take a deep breath. Focus on just the next small step. Trust that things will slowly fall into place. Overthinking creates pressure, but peace comes when you learn to let go a little.

Be patient with yourself. Give your mind a break. Sit in silence. Go for a walk. Do something simple that brings you joy. Often, the best ideas and solutions come when you stop trying so hard to find them.

Let life unfold one moment at a time. That's where calm begins.

❖ The Bridge That Was Never Broken

Arjun stood at the edge of the small wooden bridge just outside his village. The path ahead led to a job interview, an opportunity he had been preparing for months. But he couldn't move. His thoughts buzzed like bees in a jar.

What if I forget everything during the interview? What if they ask me something I don't know? What if I stumble on my words? What if they laugh?

He glanced at the bridge again. It was sturdy, built by the villagers long ago, and used by hundreds every day. But today, to Arjun, it looked suspicious. He imagined it breaking under his weight, splinters flying, him falling into the rocky stream below.

He took a step back. Minutes passed. Then hours. The sun began to set.

A little girl came skipping down the road, humming a tune. She gave Arjun a cheerful smile and walked right across the bridge without any hesitation or fear.

Arjun stared, stunned. The bridge didn't even creak.

He laughed to himself, quietly at first, then louder.

It was never the bridge that was weak. It was his fear that had built cracks where there were none.

He took a deep breath, stepped forward, and crossed.

Overthinking is like building imaginary bridges of fear over real paths of possibility. Most of the time, the danger exists only in the mind.

5. Declutter

A messy space often leads to a messy mind. When your surroundings are full of things you don't need, it can feel heavy and stressful. Start small, like clearing your table, organising a drawer, or donating things you no longer use. Even simple steps can bring a sense of calm.

But decluttering isn't just about stuff. It also means looking at your time and your relationships. Are you saying "yes" to too many things? Are there people who constantly drain your energy or bring negativity into your life?

Letting go of what no longer serves you, whether it's extra clothes, a packed schedule, or a toxic friendship. Creates space and in that space, peace can grow.

Simplicity outside helps create simplicity inside. The less you carry, the lighter you feel. Decluttering helps you breathe easier, think more clearly, and focus on what truly matters.

❖ The Room and the Mind

Meera's apartment was always full of clothes she never wore, books she never read, trinkets she didn't even remember buying. Every evening, she came home feeling strangely tired, as if the walls were closing in on her.

One Sunday morning, she decided to clear her study table so she could "think better." She started with old bills, then unused pens, then piles of papers she had been "meaning to sort." By afternoon, the table was empty except for her laptop and a single lamp.

That night, as she sat to work, she noticed that her thoughts felt lighter, like there was more space inside her head.

Encouraged, Meera began to look beyond her table. She trimmed her overflowing schedule, said no to events she didn't enjoy, and distanced herself from a friendship that had long turned bitter.

The changes were small at first, but over time her home felt airier, her calendar calmer, and her heart quieter.

She realised decluttering wasn't just about removing things, instead it was about making space for peace. And the lighter her life became on the outside, the freer she felt on the inside.

6. Gratitude

When life feels heavy, it helps to shift your focus to what's still good. Gratitude is like sunlight. It doesn't erase the darkness, but it makes it easier to see what's beautiful around you.

You don't need something big to be grateful for. It can be as small as a warm cup of tea, a kind word, a cool breeze, or simply waking up to a new day. These little things, when noticed, add up and bring lightness to your heart.

When you start to appreciate what you have, your mind slowly let's go of what you lack. The stress, the complaints, the sadness begin to lose their grip. A grateful heart naturally pushes out negativity, just like fresh air pushes out stale air from a room.

Gratitude doesn't mean ignoring your problems. It means choosing to also see the good. And the more you practice it, the more you'll find. It's a quiet but powerful way to feel better, even when life isn't perfect.

A Life Lesson from an Unknown Soul

It was the year 2021 when I took one of the boldest steps of my life. I decided to leave my stable job and pursue my dream of starting my own business.

But destiny had other plans. Soon after, the country was hit hard by the second wave of COVID-19. My entire family, including me, tested positive. It was a terrifying time. My mother's condition turned serious, and her recovery was long and painful.

During those days, there was no income. My savings, which I had built over the years to support my dream, began to disappear rapidly, not for business, but for survival. The business was crawling like a tortoise, and nothing seemed to move forward.

One day, while everything was hectic, I visited a Gurudwara seeking guidance and a moment of stillness. As I stood in line, I overheard a poor woman in front of me. She kept softly repeating the words, "Aapka lakh lakh shukrana"

Her words struck me like lightning.

Here was a woman who probably had far less than I did — and yet, she was overflowing with gratitude. In contrast, I had a roof over my head, savings in my bank, food to eat, and a family that was slowly healing, but all I could feel was worry and disappointment.

That moment was transformative. I never saw her face, I don't know her name, but she became my teacher that day. A silent teacher who reminded me that gratitude is not about what you have; it's about how you see what you have.

Since that day, I made a quiet promise to myself to thank God every single day, no matter the circumstances. Because the life I have, despite its struggles, is still a beautiful gift.

7. Stillness

In a world that constantly demands our attention, stillness is a forgotten art. We often believe that every moment must be filled with activity, noise, or productivity. But true renewal begins when we pause.

Stillness doesn't always mean meditation or sitting cross-legged with closed eyes. It can be as simple as watching the sky, sitting quietly in nature, or lying down without your phone for a few minutes. It is the act of not doing.

In moments of stillness, the mind begins to settle. The chaos of thoughts slows down, and our awareness expands. It's in this quiet space that clarity often arises, answers become visible, creativity flows, and a sense of calm begins to surface.

Nature thrives in stillness. The sun rises without rush, rivers flow without resistance, and trees stand tall without movement. We, too, are part of this rhythm. When we allow ourselves to pause, we align with this natural flow, reconnecting to something deeper than daily distractions.

Stillness isn't wasted time; it is sacred space. It is where the noise ends, and the truth begins to whisper.

❖ The Lake Without Ripples

Arjun's life was a blur of deadlines, phone calls, and rushing from one task to another. Even his weekends were filled with "things to do" lists. One day, feeling unusually drained, he wandered into a quiet park near his office.

There was a small lake there. The water was perfectly still, like a sheet of glass, reflecting the trees and clouds above. Arjun sat down on a bench to check his phone, but for some reason, he didn't.

Minutes passed. He just looked at the water. Listened to the soft rustle of leaves. Felt the sun on his face.

Slowly, his shoulders dropped. His breathing deepened. Thoughts that had been tangled all morning began to loosen, like knots coming undone. A solution to a work problem popped into his mind without effort. The anxiety he'd been carrying seemed smaller, lighter.

When he finally stood up to leave, Arjun realised something: the lake hadn't done anything. It had simply been still. And in its stillness, it had reminded him of his own.

From that day on, Arjun made it a habit to find small moments of stillness not as an escape, but as a way to return home to himself.

8. Express

Don't keep everything bottled up. Emotions, especially intense ones like sadness, anger, or confusion, need an outlet. Find someone you trust, a friend, family member, or therapist. Talk openly about what you're feeling. Sometimes, simply putting your thoughts into words can bring surprising clarity and relief.

If speaking isn't easy, writing in a journal can be just as powerful. Pour out your thoughts without judgment or editing. Your journal becomes a safe space where emotions can flow freely.

Even crying, often seen as a sign of weakness, is actually a healthy emotional release. It helps reduce stress, calms the nervous system, and allows emotional weight to lighten.

Suppressing emotions may feel like control in the short term, but over time, it creates inner pressure that can lead to emotional burnout, anxiety, or even physical symptoms. Expressing yourself is not just an emotional act; it's a form of self-care and healing. It's how you make space inside yourself for peace to return.

❖ The Teacup

For months, Neel kept telling himself he was “fine.” He smiled at work, cracked jokes with friends, and never mentioned the sleepless nights or the tight knot in his chest.

One day, he visited his grandmother. As they had tea, she poured his cup to the brim and kept pouring. Tea spilt over, running onto the saucer and table.

“Grandma, stop! It’s overflowing,” Neel said.

She smiled gently. “So are you.”

Her words sank deep. That evening, Neel called his best friend and, for the first time in a long time, spoke honestly about the stress, the loneliness, and the weight he’d been carrying.

By the end of the conversation, the knot in his chest had loosened. It didn’t solve everything, but it made the load lighter.

Neel learned that emotions, like tea, need space to be poured out or they’ll spill in ways we can’t control. And in expressing them, he made room for peace to flow back in.

9. Be In Present

It feels good when someone truly listens to you. We expect others to give us their full attention while we are talking. Similarly, it's important to be mentally and emotionally present with the person in front of us. Unfortunately, we've become so distracted that even while talking to someone, our minds are elsewhere, planning the next thing.

Stop rewinding the past or fast-forwarding to the future. Right now is the only real moment. When you're fully present, your mind stops carrying an extra load.

Emptying yourself is not a one-time act; it's a daily practice. Each time you let go of what you don't need, you make space for peace, purpose, and joy to enter.

❖ The Coffee Conversation

Riya met her old school friend, Ankit, after years. They sat in a cosy café, coffee cups warming their hands.

But as Ankit spoke about his life, Riya's mind drifted, remembering an unfinished email, wondering what she'd cook for dinner, replaying something awkward she had said earlier that week. She nodded at the right times, but deep down, she knew she wasn't *really* there.

Halfway through, Ankit paused. "You seemed far away," he said softly.

The words hit her. She realised she wanted Ankit's attention when she spoke, but she wasn't giving him the same gift. So, she took a slow breath, set her phone aside, and let her mind stop racing. She listened not just to his words, but to his tone, his expressions, the pauses between sentences.

Something shifted. The conversation felt warmer, more real. Time seemed to slow down.

When they finally parted, Riya felt lighter, as if she'd been truly *in* that moment instead of rushing past it. She realised that being present wasn't just about others, it was also a way of freeing herself from the constant noise in her own head.

Key Takeaways

Question Your Mind's Stories – Not every thought or meaning your mind creates is the truth. Pause and ask: *"Is this real, or just my mind's version?"*

Make Space Within – Like the flute, let go of ego, fear, and clutter. Emptiness creates room for peace, creativity, and soulful living.

Breathe to Slow Down – Just one deep, conscious breath can pause the rush, calm the mind, and bring you back to the present.

Release the Past with Grace – Letting go doesn't mean forgetting—it means making space for peace, love, and healing to enter.

Be the Sky, Not the Clouds – Your thoughts are passing clouds. Observe them without attachment, and clarity will emerge.

Detach from Titles and Labels – You are more than your achievements, roles, or others' opinions. Freedom comes when you stop clinging to them.

Step Out of Overthinking – Fear builds imaginary walls. Trust the path, take one step, and let clarity come with movement

Key Takeaway

Declutter Inside and Out – Simplify your space, your time, and your relationships. Less outside creates calmer inside.

Practice Daily Gratitude – Gratitude shifts focus from what's missing to what's already beautiful. It's a quiet force of healing.

Return to Stillness – Stillness isn't empty time—it's sacred space where peace, clarity, and creativity unfold naturally.

Express, Don't Suppress – Emotions need release. Speak, write, or cry—expression lightens the heart and creates space for peace.

Live in the Present Moment – Stop rewinding the past or fast-forwarding to the future. Presence is the real gift of freedom.

Chapter 7

What Blocks Your Inner Glow

Every morning, I go for a walk. The path is always full of people, some jogging, some walking, some just sitting and talking.

As I look around, I notice something on people's faces. Many carry a worried look. Some look blank, as if their mind is far away. Only a few faces seem truly alive, glowing with a light from inside.

When I see those faces, I am reminded of small children, around two or three years old. At that age, every child glows naturally. You can see it in their smile, in their eyes, in their excitement about life. Their faces are open, joyful, and full of light. So, I often ask myself, what happens as we grow older? Why does that light fade from most faces?

It took me time to understand the reason. At first, I thought life's problems, struggles, and responsibilities were the main cause. But later I realised something different.

"We are the ones who dim our own lights."

It doesn't happen all at once. It fades slowly, over time. We stop doing the little things that make us happy. We become busy chasing outer beauty, outer success, and what others think of us. We focus on looking good on the outside, and we forget to care for the inside.

But the truth is that we can't really shine on the outside if our light inside is weak or gone. After a lot of thought, I found that real inner glow depends on three things: health, knowledge, and calmness.

Think, can you be truly happy if:

- You are calm and wise, but your body is weak or sick?
- You are healthy and calm, but you don't know to make good choices?
- You are healthy and smart, but your mind is always restless and full of stress?

The answer is no. We need all three: a healthy body, a growing mind, and a peaceful heart to feel whole and to shine from within. Our glow doesn't fade because of one big problem. It fades because of many small poisons that quietly enter our lives.

Some of those poisons are:

- **Comparison** – Always looking at others and feeling like we are not enough.
- **Greed** – Never feeling satisfied with what we have, always wanting more.
- **Self-doubt** – Not trusting our own skills and decisions.
- **Resentment** – Holding on to past hurts and anger.

- **Busyness** – Filling every moment with work or distractions so we never have to sit quietly with ourselves.

These poisons start small. At first, they don't seem dangerous. But slowly, they block our natural joy and make our faces heavy and dull. The good thing is that we can bring our glow back. The very moment we notice it's missing, we have already taken the first step. The process doesn't start with expensive creams, new clothes, or a perfect social media profile. It starts with a pause.

Ask yourself

- Am I being too hard on myself?
- Am I letting others' opinions control my self-worth?
- Am I chasing things that drain me instead of things that give me peace?

There was a time when I looked successful from the outside. I was busy, meeting goals, and always surrounded by people. But inside, I felt tired and dull. I realised my health was suffering because I wasn't resting enough or eating well. My mind wasn't learning anything new, but was filled with social media and news. And I had no calmness at all because my phone and my thoughts kept me busy all the time.

Small, daily changes can bring big results. Move your body, eat food that gives you energy, read and learn something every day, and give your mind a few minutes of quiet. Say "no" to things or people that constantly take away your peace.

When I began caring for my health, feeding my mind with good knowledge, and creating time for peace, the change was slow but real. My mood lifted, my energy came back, and people even started saying, “You look different—you’re glowing.”

If you want your glow to return

1. **Care for your health** – Eat well, sleep enough, and move your body.
2. **Grow your mind** – Read, learn, ask questions, and stay curious.
3. **Protect your calmness** – Take breaks, spend time in nature, and give your mind quiet moments.

This isn’t a one-day job. Just like a lamp needs oil to keep burning, our inner light needs daily care.

In today’s world, everyone is busy polishing the outside like filters, photos, and perfect images. But if you’ve ever met someone whose presence makes you feel good, you know it’s the inner light that makes the real difference.

That light is still inside you. It may be covered by layers of stress, worry, or neglect, but it has not gone out.

Give it your attention. Feed it with health, knowledge, and calmness. And when it shines again, not only will your own life feel brighter, but you will also light up the lives of those around you.

ACADEMIY
ACNIESEMENTS

Arjun Story

Once there was a boy named Arjun. He was full of life, always smiling, helping others, and enjoying the little things. People around him often said, *"There's something special about him. He glows."*

As Arjun grew up, things changed. He started chasing good grades, better clothes, more likes on social media, and a perfect image. Slowly, he stopped doing the things that once made him happy. He laughed less, helped less, and always felt tired even when everything looked fine from the outside.

One day, Arjun looked in the mirror and thought, *"Why do I look so dull? Where is that light in my eyes?"* He tried changing his hairstyle, his clothes, and even joined a gym. But nothing worked.

One evening, he met his old school teacher, who used to say, *"Real glow comes from within."* She gently asked him, *"When was the last time you did something just for joy, not to prove anything or get approval?"* Arjun thought hard… and couldn't remember.

That night, he sat quietly and reflected. He realised he had stopped enjoying life. He was always comparing, always trying to be someone else. He had let go of his peace, his smile, and his natural glow just to fit into the world's image of success.

From the next day, Arjun began small changes like a morning walk, helping a stranger, reading a book for fun, and talking kindly to himself. Day by day, his smile returned. The glow in his eyes slowly came back.

This story of Arjun is just one example. Your life may be different. Your challenges and path may not be the same. But the message remains true for all of us.

You may have to take different steps, make different changes, or face different fears. But in the end, what really matters is that you work toward becoming happy, healthy, and wise.

No matter where you are in life, it's never too late to bring back your inner glow. Just start with small steps, stay true to yourself, and keep moving forward one day at a time.

Key Takeaways

- **Your Inner Light Fades Slowly** – Not from life's struggles, but from small habits of neglect, comparison, and self-doubt.
- **Outer Shine Can't Replace Inner Glow** – No cream, filter, or title can cover a restless mind or tired spirit.
- **Health, Knowledge, and Calmness Are the Three Pillars** – True glow needs a strong body, a curious mind, and a peaceful heart.
- **Small Poisons Block Joy** – Comparison, greed, resentment, busyness, and self-doubt quietly dim your natural radiance.
- **Awareness Is the First Step** – The moment you notice your glow is missing, you begin the journey to restore it.
- **Glow Returns Through Daily Care** – Eat well, rest enough, move often, learn daily, and make space for silence.
- **Joy Fuels Glow More Than Approval** – Do things for love, fun, and kindness—not for likes, praise, or comparison.
- **Your Light Is Still Inside You** – Stress may cover it, but it never disappears; nurture it and it will shine again.
- **When You Shine, You Spread Light** – A glowing heart not only brightens your life but uplifts everyone around you.

Notes

Chapter 8

How Story Telling Transforms Identity

Have you ever noticed how we carry around stories in our minds all day long? These stories shape how we see ourselves, how we interact with others, and how we show up in the world. Some of these stories are filled with strength and beauty, while others hold us back, dimming our light, our inner glow.

When we talk about discovering your glow, we are not just speaking of happiness or success. We are talking about remembering your truth, your wholeness, and your unique light that sometimes gets buried beneath layers of doubt, fear, pain, and untrue stories.

We Are All Storytellers

From the moment we are born, we begin to build our sense of self. We collect moments, reactions, words from others, and experiences. Slowly, these become stories:

- "I was always the quiet one."
- "I'm not good at public speaking."
- "I never finish what I start."
- "I have to prove myself to be loved."

Each of these becomes a part of how we define ourselves. Sometimes they serve us. Many times, they don't. But the truth is that we are not the stories, we are the storytellers.

And when we take charge of the story, we take charge of our identity.

How Stories Shape Our Glow

Our inner glow is that quiet confidence, that sense of ease, joy, and purpose that lives inside all of us. But as we grow older, life throws challenges at us, and we often begin to tell ourselves different stories:

- "Life is a struggle."
- "I am too old to change."
- "Success is for others, not me."

These beliefs begin to define our identity. They affect our choices, our relationships, and our dreams. We dim our light trying to fit in, trying to please, trying to survive. We forget our own shine.

But when we start to become aware of the story we are telling and we begin to question it, something powerful happens. Awareness is the first spark that reignites our glow.

The Power of Rewriting Your Story

Let's say you've been telling yourself, "I always fail." That story likely came from a painful experience it may be a failed exam, a lost job, a broken relationship. But the story you choose to hold onto becomes your identity.

"Yes, I failed before, but I learned. I grew. I am still trying. That means I'm brave."

This simple change in story does more than shift your mood; it shifts your energy. Your glow begins to return.

You don't need to pretend bad things didn't happen. You don't need to lie to yourself. You only need to look at the full picture and permit yourself to grow beyond the past.

The Healing Magic of Sharing Your Story

Storytelling doesn't just live in your head. Sharing it out loud through speaking, writing, art, or even quiet reflection helps release the weight.

When you tell your story with honesty and kindness, you:

- Heal old wounds.
- Find meaning in your pain.
- Inspire others who are walking similar paths.

You might think, "Why would anyone care about my story?" But stories are the bridges that connect us. They help us see we're not alone. They open hearts. They start with a change in others and in ourselves.

Everyone's Story Is Unique

Your story may not look like Arjun's (from the earlier chapter). You may not have faced the same losses or victories. Your challenges, lessons, and joys are unique to you.

That's why there is no single solution to discovering your glow. For some, it might take stepping into nature. For others, it could mean healing a broken relationship, taking a new risk, or simply resting.

But every path begins with becoming aware of the story you're living and choosing whether you want to keep it or rewrite it.

What Dims Our Glow Over Time?

Let's talk about the poisons that creep into our stories and identities:

- **Comparison**: The moment we measure ourselves against someone else, we often shrink. We forget our own value.
- **Greed**: Always wanting more can make us blind to what we already have.
- **Self-doubt**: That small voice that says, "You're not enough," can become a loud story if we let it.
- **Guilt and shame**: Carrying mistakes from the past can make us feel unworthy of love or success.

These poisons don't enter all at once. They slip in slowly, quietly. But if we're not careful, they become part of the story we live by.

The good news is that you can begin fresh at any moment.

Exercises to Discover and Rewrite Your Story

1. **Journal:** Write down a story you've been telling yourself that feels heavy or limiting.

- Where did it come from?
- Is it really true?
- How would you tell it if you were your own best friend?

2. **Mirroring:** Stand in front of a mirror and speak a new story:
    - "I am healing."
    - "I am learning."
    - "I am becoming who I'm meant to be."
3. **Speaking:** Share a personal story of struggle and how you came through it, even a little bit. Either with friends or with yourself. Let the story remind you of your strength.

Closing Reflection: Your Glow Lives in the Story You Choose to Tell

You are not broken. You are becoming.

The glow you're looking for is not in the mirror, the bank account, or the applause. It is already inside you waiting for your attention, your love, and your truth.

Start with your story. Speak it. Shape it. Let it grow with you. And as your story changes, so will your identity. So will your glow.

Because your glow is not lost, it is just waiting to be remembered.

Let today be the day you begin a new chapter. One where you are the hero. One where your light shines through.

STORYTELLING – Rewriting Your Identity

Practice: Hero's Journal

- Choose one difficult event in your past.
- Now write it as a story where you are the hero:

Action Item	Response
What was the challenge?	
What did you learn?	
How did you grow stronger?	
Summarise: *"If this were a chapter in my life book, what would you call it?"*	

Key Takeaways

You Are Not the story, You Are the Storyteller – Your past events don't define you; your interpretation does.

Stories Shape Identity – What you keep repeating ("I'm not enough," "I can't change") becomes how you see yourself.

Awareness Sparks Transformation – The moment you notice a limiting story, your glow begins to return.

Rewriting Changes Energy – A new story like "I am learning, I am brave" shifts not just your mood but your entire presence.

Sharing Heals – Speaking your story out loud can release pain, inspire others, and connect hearts.

Poisons Hide in Stories – Comparison, greed, guilt, and self-doubt silently dim your glow until you rewrite them.

Every Story Is Unique – Your glow doesn't come from copying others, but from honouring your own path.

Your Glow Lives in Your Story – The light you seek isn't outside—it grows in the story you choose to tell yourself every day.

You Can Begin a New Chapter Anytime – Identity isn't fixed; you can always step into a fresh story where you are the hero.

Notes

PART - 3

LIVING RADIANTLY AND SHARING THE LIGHT

Chapter 9

The Science Behind Mind-Body Balance

Let's pause for a moment and imagine the sun.

The sun shines because atoms inside it fuse with unimaginable energy. This process, called fusion, produces the warmth and light that make life possible on Earth. Without this joining of atoms, the world would be dark, cold, and lifeless.

Now, think of yourself. You are not made of exploding stars, but you do have your own kind of atoms, say **inner atoms** that can combine to release a glow just as powerful. Not a glow of heat and fire, but of **presence, joy, and inner strength**.

This glow is not physical light but an energy others can feel. It's in the calmness of your words, the warmth of your smile, the patience in your responses, and the strength in your choices.

And just like the sun needs fusion, you need your **inner atoms** to fuse together in harmony.

The Health Atom: Your Foundation

The first and most important atom is **Health**.

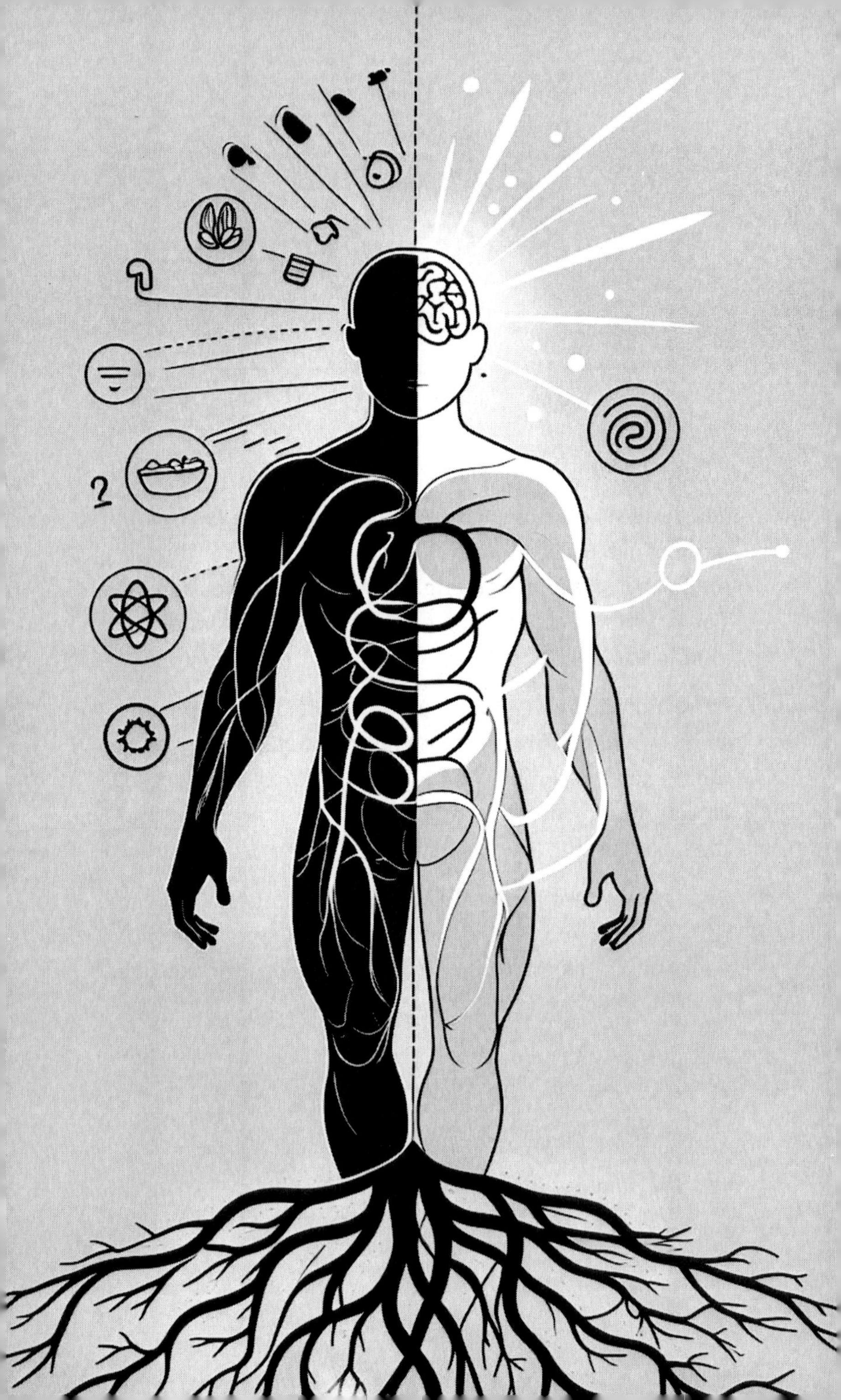

A strong mind cannot live in a weak body for long. Imagine trying to carry a bucket with a broken handle. It doesn't matter how much water you put in; it will spill. Similarly, without health, even your biggest dreams can't hold together.

Health doesn't mean only the absence of illness. It means

- Eating foods that nourish instead of drain you.
- Moving your body so that energy flows freely.
- Rest deeply so your body repairs itself.
- Breathing fully so oxygen becomes fuel for your cells.

Think of your body as the **soil**. You may have the best seeds (dreams, plans, knowledge), but without fertile soil, nothing grows.

When you respect your body, you are telling yourself: *"I want to live fully. I want my life to have the energy it deserves."*

The Knowledge Atom: Nourishment for the Mind

Once your foundation is strong, you need nourishment for your mind. This is where the **Knowledge Atom** comes in.

Knowledge is not just about books, degrees, or certificates. True knowledge is about being a **student of life**. It's about staying curious, asking *"Why?"* and *"What can I learn here?"*.

When the mind is hungry and you feed it junk like constant scrolling, gossip, or shallow information, it feels busy but stays empty. When you feed it with reflection, wisdom, and meaningful ideas, it grows sharp and clear.

Knowledge also teaches you perspective. Imagine two people stuck in a traffic jam

- One gets angry, honks, and raises their blood pressure.
- The other takes a breath, turns on calming music, and thinks, *"Maybe this is life's way of slowing me down."*

Both are in the same situation, but knowledge allows the second person to choose peace over frustration.

When **Health and Knowledge** combine, your actions become wise and intentional. You don't just react; you respond with awareness.

The Calmness Atom: Anchor in the Storm

But even with health and knowledge, something can still feel missing. That missing piece is **Calmness**.

Calmness is your **anchor**. Life will always bring storms such as stress at work, misunderstandings in relationships, and uncertainty about the future. Without calmness, you drift like a boat without direction.

Calmness does not mean you never feel upset. It means you have the strength to pause, breathe, and not let chaos control you.

Imagine pouring water into a glass that is constantly shaking. The water will always spill. But when the glass is steady, it can hold whatever is poured into it. Calmness makes you that steady glass.

- It lets you think clearly when others panic.
- It helps you respond with patience when others react with anger.
- It allows you to protect your peace, even in noise.

Without calmness, health can turn into obsession, and knowledge can turn into overthinking. With calmness, both become balanced and beautiful.

Now comes the magic. When **Health**, **Knowledge**, and **Calmness** combine with intention, they create something I call your **Personal Fusion**.

This inner fusion doesn't explode like the sun; it glows

- It glows in your smile, which feels genuine and comforting.
- It glows in your decisions, which are thoughtful and wise.
- It glows in your presence, which people notice even when you're silent.

This glow is not about outer beauty. It's about **inner alignment**. A balance between body, mind, and soul.

It is a glow of

- **Happiness**, because you live in harmony.
- **Confidence**, because you know your worth.
- **Patience**, because you trust the process.
- **Self-respect**, because you honour your needs.

This glow is the quiet power that makes people say, *"There's something about you."*

I call it the **Emotional Selfish Bond**.

It's the bond you create with yourself when you choose your well-being without harming others. Often, we think being selfish is bad. But there's a positive kind of selfishness that is essential for balance.

It means

- Saying **"No"** when something drains you, without guilt.
- Caring for your health today, not waiting for a doctor's warning.
- Feeding your mind with wisdom, not just approval from others.
- Creating quiet time for yourself, even if people call it "selfish."
- Guarding your peace like a sacred space.

This bond is like the invisible glue that holds your three atoms together. Without it, you scatter your energy everywhere. With it, you shine.

Reflection Pause

Take a moment and ask yourself:

- Am I feeding my **Health Atom** with real care?
- Am I feeding my **Knowledge Atom** with wisdom, not just noise?
- Am I feeding my **Calmness Atom** with stillness and peace?
- Do I protect my energy with a healthy bond to myself?

Your answers are not just reflections, instead they are the **science of your glow**.

Notes

Chapter 10

Interview-style reflections with others

Sometimes, the best way to find your missing glow is by borrowing someone else's mirror for a while.

Life has phases where everything feels dull. You wake up, do what's needed, but inside, something feels switched off. Your spark seems to have gone on a vacation without telling you. In those moments, try sitting with another person and asking questions not like "How are you?" or "What's up?" but questions that go deeper.

Think of it like hosting your own little podcast at home. You're not Oprah. You don't need a stage, a camera, or millions of viewers. All you need is curiosity. Because in the right kind of conversation, you don't just learn about the other person, but you discover forgotten parts of yourself.

Every human being carries a library inside them. Their joys, struggles, mistakes, lessons, fears, and dreams are like chapters waiting to be read. And when you take time to ask and truly listen, you find wisdom you never expected. That's the power of interview-style reflections.

In our fast world, we spend hours scrolling through people's lives on screens, but hardly pause to enter someone's real inner world. We know what our friends ate for lunch, but we don't know what keeps them awake at night. We send emojis but often miss emotions.

This is why interview-style reflections matter. When you sit with someone and say, "Tell me about a moment that changed you," you're giving them a priceless gift: the feeling of being heard. And in return, you receive something too, maybe a lesson, maybe hope, maybe a reminder that you're not alone in your struggles.

These conversations can help you

- See life through new eyes
- Understand your own values better
- Feel less alone in your experiences
- Strengthen bonds with people
- Grow in empathy and awareness

It's almost like watering a plant. The other person blossoms when they're heard, and so do you.

How to Begin an Interview-Style Reflection

The good news is that you don't need anything fancy to start. No microphones, no notes, no spotlight. Just presence. Just curiosity.

You can begin with anyone, maybe a parent, grandparent, sibling, friend, mentor, or colleague. All you need is a safe, quiet space where you both can speak without rush or distraction.

Here are some gentle, open-ended questions to try

- "What's one life lesson you learned the hard way?"
- "When in life did you feel most proud of yourself?"
- "What was a turning point in your journey?"
- "What advice would you give your younger self?"
- "What helps you stay calm in tough times?"
- "What does happiness mean to you?"
- "Was there a time you felt lost? How did you find your way?"

Notice how these questions aren't about facts ("Where did you work?") but about feelings and meaning. That's what makes them powerful.

The Art of Listening

Asking the question is just the beginning. The real magic is in listening.

When someone opens their heart, don't rush to fill the silence. Let them think. Let them pause. Let them share at their own pace.

Listen not just with your ears, but with your eyes and your heart. Pay attention to their tone, their pauses, even the words they struggle to find. Don't jump in with solutions unless they ask. Sometimes the most healing thing you can do is to simply hold space. Silence is not empty. Silence is where the deeper truths live.

What You Might Discover

These conversations often surprise us. You might learn things about people you thought you knew well:

- Your quiet mother might reveal a story of courage she never shared before.
- A friend may admit they've been carrying silent pain behind their smile.
- A colleague might share dreams you never knew they had.
- A grandparent could tell you about choices that shaped their life in ways you never imagined.

And while listening, you'll also discover yourself. Certain stories will resonate, stirring your own memories. Certain lessons will echo in your heart, showing you what matters to you.

Reflection, when shared, is like a mirror. Through someone else's story, you see your own reflection more clearly.

Make It a Habit

The beauty of interview-style reflections is that they don't need to be rare events. You can make them a part of daily life. Over dinner, during a walk, on a long drive, or during a quiet evening, ask a deeper question.

Instead of "How was your day?" try "What made you smile today?"

Instead of "What's new?" try "What's something you've been thinking about a lot lately?"

When you make space for these conversations regularly, relationships deepen. Trust grows. Awareness expands. And your inner glow becomes warmer, grounded, and more real.

Here's a simple practice:

- Choose one person this week.
- Sit with them for 20–30 minutes.
- Ask three meaningful questions.
- Don't interrupt. Don't judge. Just listen.

Then, take a few minutes alone to reflect. Ask yourself:

- What did I learn about them?
- What did I learn about myself?

You'll realise something profound: Every person is a living book. And every conversation is a page worth reading. Some pages make you laugh, some bring tears, some awaken courage, and some remind you of love.

And once you experience this, you'll see that interview-style reflections aren't just about others. They're about reconnecting with yourself.

Closing Thought

When we stop to truly listen, we build bridges not just to another person's heart, but also back to our own.

The glow you're searching for may not come from meditation apps or motivational videos alone. Sometimes, it comes from simply sitting across from someone, asking a gentle question, and letting their story remind you of your own light.

Because when we pause long enough to hear the stories around us, we also begin to hear the voice inside us.

Notes

Chapter 11

Habits Of People Who Radiate from Within

Some people walk into a room, and you can feel their presence. They may not be loud. They may not be wearing expensive clothes. But something about them feels *bright*, *warm*, and *real*. These are people who **radiate from within**. They glow not because of what they have but because of who they are.

This kind of glow comes from inside. It is not built in a day. It is the result of habits, small daily choices and ways of living that keep their hearts open, minds calm, and souls nourished. If you want to shine like that, you can. These habits are not reserved for a lucky few. They're available to anyone, including you.

1. They Start Their Day with Intention

People who radiate from within don't just jump into the chaos of the day. They take a few quiet moments in the morning to ground themselves. It might be a prayer, a few deep breaths, a stretch, or simply sitting in silence. They ask themselves, *"What kind of energy do I want to bring today?"* This small act sets the tone for their entire day.

STARTING THE DAY WITH INTENTION
SPEAKING CARE KINDLY TO THERSELVES AND OTHERS
GRATITUDE EVERY DAY
KNOWING WHEN TO LET GO
CHOSING GROWTH OVER PERFECTION
CREATING SPACE FOR SILENCE
KEEPING THEIR CIRCLE UPLIFTING
LIVING WITH PURPOSE, NOT PRESSURE
CELEBRATING WITHOUT REASON

2. They Take Care of Their Energy, Not Just Their Looks

Yes, they may care about their appearance, but they care more about how they *feel* on the inside. They rest when tired. They move their body. They drink water. They choose food that fuels them. They protect their peace like it's gold. Because they know: when your energy is clean, your presence speaks louder than your words.

3. They Speak Kindly to Themselves and Others

Their inner dialogue is gentle. They are not harsh or critical with themselves. When they make mistakes, they learn instead of blaming. And this kindness spills into how they speak to others. They lift people. They smile often. They listen deeply. Their words feel like sunshine.

4. They Are Grateful Every Single Day

They don't take small joys for granted. A cup of tea, a quiet sunset, a kind word, they notice and feel thankful. Gratitude is not just a feeling for them; it's a habit. And this habit makes their heart feel full, even when life is imperfect.

5. They Know When to Let Go

Instead of holding on to anger, comparison, or guilt, they know how to let go. They forgive not always because others deserve it, but because they deserve peace. They don't carry emotional weight that isn't theirs. That's how they stay light. That's how they keep glowing.

6. They Choose Growth Over Perfection

They don't try to appear perfect. They are not afraid to be real, to be seen, or to admit, *"I'm still learning."* They invest time in growing reading, reflecting, and asking questions. They don't want to be better than others. They just want to be better than they were yesterday.

7. They Create Space for Silence

They are not afraid of silence. In fact, they value it. In quiet moments, they connect with themselves. They listen to their heart. They recharge. They don't always need noise, people, or screens. Silence becomes their strength.

8. They Live with Purpose, Not Pressure

They don't chase what others chase just to fit in. They follow what feels right to their soul. They may not always have a fixed plan, but they have a direction. They live with meaning. Every small act, whether it's a job, a conversation, or a walk in nature, feels connected to something deeper. That gives them a sense of calm that people can feel.

9. They Keep Their Circle Uplifting

They don't spend their energy on negativity or gossip. They value honest, uplifting company or their own company. They would rather be alone than be surrounded by people who drain them. And because they are kind and real, they naturally attract others who shine the same way.

10. They Celebrate, Even Without a Reason

They don't wait for big success to feel proud or happy. They celebrate small wins, getting through a hard day, completing a task, being kind when they could've been cold. Their joy isn't loud, but it's steady. They carry it with them like a quiet light always there, always glowing.

You might be wondering why it is important to understand the habits of individuals who radiate a powerful energy from within. The reason is simple that by recognising these traits, you gain a clear vision of the kind of person you are capable of becoming once you begin applying the practices discussed earlier and generating your own inner atoms of strength. Imagine how others will perceive you. How will they recognise the transformation in your presence, the positivity you radiate, and the calm confidence you carry. Consider the conversations people will have about you, the respect you will naturally command, and the inspiration you will spark in those around you. This awareness not only motivates you but also gives you a glimpse of the remarkable potential that lies ahead once you embark on this journey.

Chapter 12

Let Your Light Keep Glowing

This kind of bond with yourself doesn't grow in a single day. It's not like making instant noodles or getting next-day delivery from Amazon. It's something you slowly build with small, everyday actions that quietly say, "I matter."

Sometimes, that action is as simple as going to bed at 10 PM. Other times, it's deciding, "Nope, I'm skipping that noisy WhatsApp family group call today as self-care comes first."

The more you respect this bond, the more your body and mind stay charged and connected. Your glow becomes brighter even if your boss thinks it's just the reflection from your computer screen. This isn't a catchy quote to print on a mug. It's a real-life habit, something you practise daily, sometimes forget, but always return to because it's worth it.

Inside you, there's a special light. It's not from makeup, a ring light, or an expensive spa treatment. It comes from feeling alive, calm, and connected to your real self. You can't buy it. No one can send it to you in a message. It's quiet, but strong. This light is your energy, your peace, and your strength. And like a small flame, it needs care. It needs you.

No

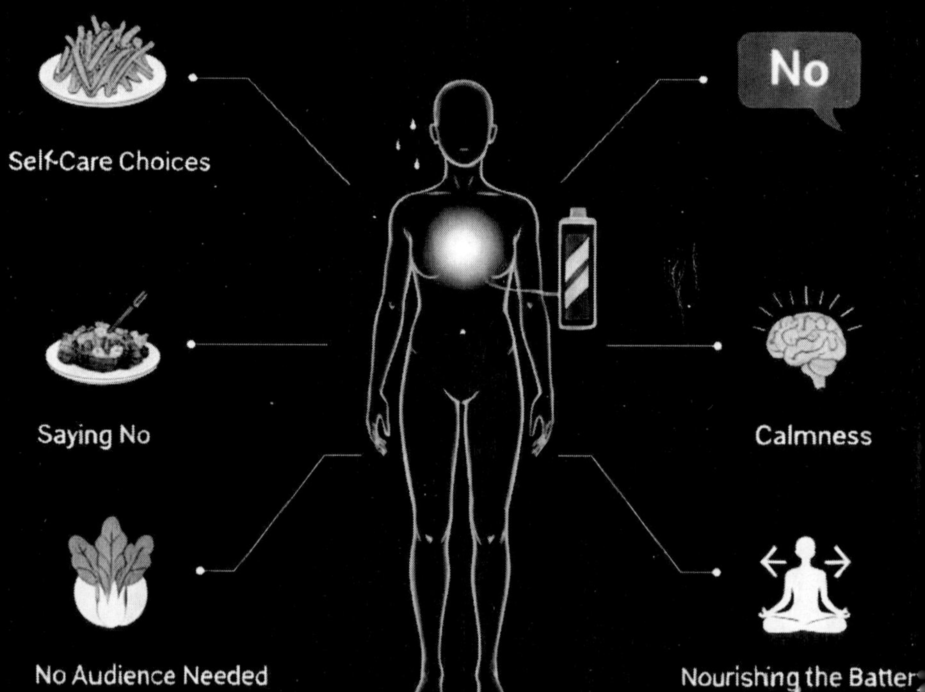
No
Self-Care Choices
Saying No
Calmness
No Audience Needed
Nourishing the Batter

Let me tell you about *Amit Uncle*. Every morning, he does yoga on his terrace wearing a vest that he retired ten years ago. He looks like he's wrestling with invisible snakes, but he swears it keeps his glow alive. "No one messes with me after Surya Namaskar," he says with a wink. Honestly, his glow might just be sweat, but it's **his**. That's the point.

Your inner light doesn't magically appear one fine morning like a Bollywood makeover scene. It's built, slowly and lovingly, through acts of self-care: choosing a salad over fried food (or at least adding the salad as decoration), breathing instead of screaming at traffic, or simply stretching without groaning like a haunted cupboard.

Every time you do something kind for yourself, like just saying "no" to another Zoom meeting, saying, "I matter." It's a small victory. And trust me, those victories pile up.

Too many people wait for applause before they shine. But here's the secret that **you don't need an audience** to glow. You don't have to earn your worth like a reality show contestant. You only need one thing: the **choice** to keep showing up for yourself. Even on bad hair days. Even when the coffee tastes weird. Even when your family doesn't understand what "me time" means.

Think of your life as a battery, and your glow is your charge. To keep it full, you need to nourish three crucial parts:

YOUR HEALTH FOCUS

VS

MIND CALMNESS

1. **Your health** (Eat veggies. Or at least stop pretending French fries are a vegetable.)
2. **Your mind** (Read something that isn't just memes.)
3. **Your calmness** (Take deep breaths. Not just sighs of frustration.)

When these roots are strong, your glow becomes steady like that one tube light in your house that never flickers, no matter what.

Some may call this "selfish." Honestly, they're probably just jealous they didn't think of it first. This isn't about ignoring the world. It's about not ignoring **yourself**. You become your own safe space, a place where you are heard, respected, and occasionally offered a hot cup of self-awareness.

You might not see results immediately. It's not magic. It's gardening. Slow. Often dirty. But deeply rewarding. Each pause, each boundary you set, each moment you laugh (even if it's just at your own texts in the mirror), is a seed. And these seeds grow into a kind of light that no storm can put out.

And please don't be too serious. Laugh often. Once, I tried meditation while playing whale music and fell asleep within three minutes, drooling on my yoga mat. It was still progress. Don't aim for perfection. Aim for **presence**.

So, wherever you are in life, feeling on top of the world or buried under to-do lists, **come home to yourself.** You're not lost. You're just being redirected to the real you. Remember who you are. (No, not your job title or your social media bio.) You're someone who deserves peace, growth, joy and the freedom to shine from the inside out.

Let the world do what it does. Let people hustle, scroll, and judge.

You? You keep glowing.

Notes

Notes

Notes

Notes